Best walks in Southern Wales

By the same author for Constable

*A Cambrian Way*
*A guide to the Cleveland Way*
*A guide to the Cotswold Way*
*Holding the heights*
*Best walks in North Wales*

# Best walks in Southern Wales

Richard Sale

Constable London

First published in Great Britain 1990
by Constable and Company Limited
3 The Lanchesters
162 Fulham Palace Road
London W6 9ER
Copyright © 1990 Richard Sale
ISBN 0 09 469110 X
Set in Times 9pt by
Carreg Limited, Nailsea, Bristol
Printed and bound in Great Britain by
The Bath Press, Avon

A CIP catalogue record for this book
is available from the British Library

# Contents

# Illustrations

(*Photographs taken by Richard Sale*)

# Maps

# Acknowledgements

I would like to thank the staff of the National Library of Wales, Aberystwyth for their considerable assistance during the research for parts of this book.

I thank Kevin Bassindale, Jan, Roger and Alan Francis and Susan Shorland for their assistance on the walks, and Philip Smith and Susan Shorland for their assistance with route mapping.

I thank Dave of The Printworks for all his help with the processing and printing of my films.

All photographs in this book were taken with Pentax camera equipment.

# Introduction

This companion volume to *Best Walks in North Wales* uses the same selection criteria as were applied for that first volume. The three dozen routes have therefore been selected to explore the variation of scenery that southern Wales has to offer, from sea cliff, through wooded river valley and forest, to bare mountain, and to include some of the most attractive features on offer, from waterfall to mountain lake.

The routes do not concentrate on the mountains of the Brecon Beacons National Park, the area's most distinctive large scale feature, although walks within the Park form a high proportion of the routes, nor do they seek out 'unspoilt' countryside. Rather they explore the history of man in the area, from earliest times to the Celts, those folk whose name is now synonymous with Welsh history, from the Welsh princes to the industries that exploited the mineral wealth of the Principality.

Most of the routes are circular. Exceptions exist only where to have 'bent' a route would have affected its character. In these (very few) cases suggestions on transport are made.

Finally, while every effort has been made to produce comprehensive and intelligible descriptions, and to back these up with equally clear maps, it must be emphasised that these should not be seen as anything but a supplement to possession of the maps mentioned at the start of each walk. Should you go off route, for whatever reason, only possession of the correct map will assist you back on to the correct line, or back to your transport.

STRUCTURE OF BOOK

Because the area covered by the book is a large one, the walks have not been grouped together by category (see below for a definition of the walk categories), but by area or hill range. To help with a choice of route in the appropriate category, all the walks are given at the end of this section in increasing order of difficulty, i.e. the easiest first, the most difficult last.

Each of the areas or hill ranges is dealt with in a separate chapter, and the introduction to each chapter deals briefly with the particular historical, geographical or geological aspects of the area. In addition there is a section (see 'Setting the Scene') that deals with the history of Wales, and southern Wales in particular, which will help relate a walk to the history of a particular area.

The walks have been divided into three categories, Easy, Intermediate and Difficult, the divisions making allowance not only for the time that a walk takes, but also for the terrain it crosses, and for the amount, and severity, of any climbing it involves. In broad terms, an Easy walk will take about two hours, an Intermediate walk up to twice as long, a good half-day's outing, while a Difficult walk will take more than about four hours and will, for most people, be a long half-day's, or day's, outing. As will be seen from the table of walks at the end of this section there are also a handful of walks that lie on the border between the categories. Those that lie between Easy and Intermediate are walks that cover easy ground, but take rather longer than other Easy walks without really warranting the higher classification. Those that lie between Intermediate and Difficult cover rough ground with few landmarks, but are, relatively, short and flat.

The time given to each walk has been calculated using Naismith's Formula, a well-known walking aid, which allows one hour for each 5 map-kilometres (3 map-miles) covered by an unladen walker and adds half an hour for each 300 m (1000 ft) of ascent. For most people this formula will under-estimate the time taken on a walk, and the under-estimation will increase as the time given for a walk increases. The reasons for this are several: firstly, no one will complete a walk in route-march style, but will pause occasionally to admire the view or watch the wildlife, and no allowance for these stops has been made; secondly, the formula makes no allowance for the roughness or otherwise of the terrain or for the effects of the weather; thirdly, no allowance has been made for rest stops, and these may be both more frequent and longer on the longer walks; and finally, the formula assumes that the walker can maintain his level of performance indefinitely. While some people can maintain 'Naismith' walking for many hours at a stretch, many, especially those new to mountain walking, tire quickly and find not only that their rest stops increase and become longer but that they cover less ground while they are actually moving.

*It is imperative, therefore, that the reader should use the walk-times as a guide only, and that newcomers to the area or to the sport should attempt lower-graded walks initially, and compare their actual performance with the given walk-time in order to gauge how long the more difficult walks will take them.*

THE WALKS

| Name/Area/Number | Length in miles | Ascent in feet | Time in hours | Terrain and special difficulties |
|---|---|---|---|---|
| **EASY** | | | | |
| Cwmystwyth Elenydd (5b) | $1\frac{1}{2}$ | Flat | $\frac{1}{2}$ | Paths. |
| The Afon Ystwyth Elenydd (5a) | 1 | 60 | $\frac{1}{2}$ | Grass, occasionally boggy. |
| Blaenafon The Valleys (32) | $2\frac{1}{2}$ | 130 | 1 | Roads. |
| Dinas Elenydd (8) | 2 | 200 | 1 | Paths, some very stony and uneven. |
| Castlemartin Pembrokeshire (12a) | $3\frac{3}{4}$ | Flat | $1\frac{1}{4}$ | Paths (within a danger area). |
| The Hyddgen Valley Plynlimon (2) | 4 | 150 | $1\frac{1}{2}$ | Paths, stony. |
| The Monmouthshire and Brecon Canal Abergavenny (31) | $4\frac{1}{2}$ | 200 | $1\frac{3}{4}$ | Paths. |
| The Cothi Valley Elenydd (7) | $3\frac{3}{4}$ | 200 | $1\frac{3}{4}$ | Roads and indistinct paths on grass. |
| Llyn y Fan Fach Mynydd Ddu (16) | 3 | 800 | $1\frac{3}{4}$ | Path. |
| Forest Sculpture The Wye Valley and the Forest of Dean (35) | 5 | 200 | 2 | Paths. |
| Bosherston Lily Ponds Pembrokeshire (12b) | 5 | 200 | 2 | Paths and road. |

| Name/Area/Number | Length in miles | Ascent in feet | Time in hours | Terrain and special difficulties |
|---|---|---|---|---|
| **EASY** | | | | |
| Skirrid Mountain Abergavenny (30) | $3^3/_4$ | 975 | 2 | Paths, some steep. |
| Water-Break-Its-Neck Radnor Forest (9) | 4 | 450 | 2 | Paths, some indistinct, and roads. |
| Mynydd Troed Black Mountains (25) | 5 | 1150 | $2^1/_2$ | Paths and grass. |
| Boughrood The Wye Valley and the Forest of Dean (33) | $6^1/_4$ | 100 | $2^1/_2$ | Road and paths. |
| **EASY/INTERMEDIATE** | | | | |
| Symonds Yat The Wye Valley and the Forest of Dean (34) | 5 | 600 | 2 | Paths, some steep. |
| The Teifi Pools Elenydd (6) | $4^1/_2$ | 160 | 2 | Paths and rough grass, occasionally boggy. |
| Carreg Cennen Mynydd Ddu (14) | 5 | 800 | $2^1/_2$ | Paths, some indistinct. |
| **INTERMEDIATE** | | | | |
| Caves and Waterfalls Forest Fawr (18) | 5 | 500 | 2 | Paths, some stony others very steep. |
| Penrhiw-Wen Elenydd (4) | 7 | 500 | 3 | Paths and pathless rough grass. |

| Name/Area/Number | Length in miles | Ascent in feet | Time in hours | Terrain and special difficulties |
|---|---|---|---|---|
| EASY/INTERMEDIATE | | | | |
| Owain Glyndwr's Way Plynlimon (3) | 8 | 1000 | $3^1/_2$ | Paths and pathless grass, some steep slopes. |
| Rhosili Gower (13) | $5^1/_2$ | 650 | $3^1/_2$ | Paths, some at cliff edge. Very rough if the crossing to Worm's Head is made. |
| St David's Pembrokeshire (10) | 9 | 300 | $3^1/_2$ | Paths. |
| The Grwyne Fawr Valley Black Mountains (28) | $7^1/_2$ | 1650 | $4^1/_2$ | Paths and tracks. |
| INTERMEDIATE/DIFFICULT | | | | |
| The Llangattock Quarries Llangattock Escarpment (24) | 6 | 650 | $2^1/_2$ | Paths and rough moor. |
| Chartists' Cave Llangattock Escarpment (23) | 7 | 800 | 3 | Rough moor. |
| Tommy Jones Memorial Walk Brecon Beacons (19) | 6 | 1600 | $3^3/_4$ | Paths. |
| DIFFICULT | | | | |
| The Preseli Hills Pembrokeshire (11) | 10 | 1150 | 4 | Paths, some indistinct. ( Information for one-way traverse.) |
| Bryn Teg Brecon Beacons (21) | 9 | 2130 | $4^1/_2$ | Paths. |

| Name/Area/Number | Length in miles | Ascent in feet | Time in hours | Terrain and special difficulties |
|---|---|---|---|---|
| **DIFFICULT** | | | | |
| Llanthony Priory Black Mountains (29) | 10 | 1400 | $4^1/_2$ | Paths and tracks. |
| The Horns of Mynydd Ddu Mynydd Ddu (17) | 9 | 2500 | $4^1/_2$ | Paths, sometimes indistinct or non-existent, over rough moor. |
| The Eastern Beacons Brecon Beacons (22) | $7^1/_2$ | 1800 | $4^1/_2$ | Paths. |
| The Neuadd Reservoirs Brecon Beacons (20) | 10 | 2450 | 5 | Paths. |
| Waun Fach Black Mountains (26) | 10 | 2450 | 5 | Paths and rough moor. |
| Table Mountain Black Mountains (27) | $11^1/_4$ | 2250 | 5 | Paths. |
| Deepest Mynydd Ddu Mynydd Ddu (15) | 9 | 1650 | 4 | Paths, sometimes indistinct or non-existent, over barren moor. (Information for one-way traverse.) |
| Pen Pumlumon Fawr Plynlimon (1) | $10^1/_2$ | 1630 | $5^1/_2$ | Paths, some indistinct. Some rough ground. (The 'official' walk is shorter.) |
| Lower Wye The Wye Valley and the Forest of Dean (36) | $12^1/_2$ | 1650 | 5 | Paths, some steep. |

## THE WELSH LANGUAGE

The Celtic language that crossed to Britain from continental Europe split into two variants, the Goidelic language occurring in Ireland, Scotland and the Isle of Man, the Brythonic language in Wales and Cornwall. The two variants are now differentiated as 'Q Celtic' – Goidelic Celtic or Gaelic – and 'P Celtic' – Welsh, Cornish and the similar language of Brittany, Breton. The reason for the definition is in the pronunciation of 'qu'. Q Celtic pronounces this as 'c', while P Celtic pronounces it as 'p'. An easy illustration is the difference in the word for mountain. Welsh has *pen*, while Gaelic has *ceann*.

To the English eye the Welsh language is an unreadable mass of vowel-less words, consonants back-to-back. This impression is based on the misconception that the alphabets of the two languages are the same. In fact Welsh has extra consonants, 'dd', 'll' and ff' being letters – not as strange as it seems, for remember that English has 'w', i.e. uu – and can utilise 'w' and 'y' as vowels. While 'dd' and 'll' have their own sounds – the former as 'th'; the latter as 'thl' – 'ff' is pronounced 'f', the Welsh 'f' being pronounced 'v'. Thus Tryfan is pronounced 'Tryvaen' and *cwm* (a corrie or mountain hollow) is pronounced 'coom'. A second, and radical, departure from English is initial mutation, the alteration of the initial consonants of words when the final sound of the preceding word is of particular form. The reason for this appears to be straightforwardly aesthetic. However the (apparently random) interchangeability of, say, *fawr* and *mawr* (large) or *fach* and *bach* (small), not to mention other worse forms, e.g. *cam – gam – ngham – cham*, makes the casual observer wince.

Throughout the book the common form of place-names has been used, even when this has meant using an English version rather than the orthodox Welsh. Thus, for instance, the eastern range of hills in the Brecon Beacons National Park has been called Mynydd Ddu rather than Black Mountain (no final 's') or Carmarthen Van, while the western arm has been called the Black Mountains (with a final 's').

An attempt at a comprehensive glossary of useful Welsh words is obviously doomed to failure, but the following is, I hope, a useful short list, to allow the walker to better understand the ground being traversed.

*Aber*, confluence, but usually a river mouth
*Afon*, river
*Allt (Gallt)*, hill, especially if wooded
*Bach (Fach, Bychan)*, small
*Bedd*, grave
*Betws*, chapel
*Blaen*, head of valley
*Bont*, bridge
*Braich*, arm
*Bwlch,* pass
*Cadair*, chair
*Caer*, fort
*Capel*, chapel
*Carn (Carnedd)*, a pile of stones
*Carreg*, stone
*Castell*, castle
*Cau*, deep hollow
*Cefn*, ridge
*Clogwyn*, cliff
*Coch (Goch)*, red
*Coed*, wood
*Craig*, crag
*Crib*, comb, narrow ridge
*Cwm*, mountain hollow, a valley with a backslope, as in the famous
    usage in Western Cwm below Everest
*Dinas*, town or hill-fort
*Du (Ddu)*, black
*Dwr*, water
*Dyffryn*, valley
*Eglwys*, church
*Eira*, snow
*Esgair*, long ridge
*Ffordd*, road, pathway
*Ffynnon*, well, spring
*Glas (Las)*, blue-green
*Gribin*, jagged ridge
*Gwyn*, white

*Gwynt*, wind
*Hafod*, summer dwelling, hillside house for summer use
*Hen*, old
*Hendre*, winter dwelling, valley house for winter use
*Hir*, long
*Isaf*, lowest
*Llech*, flat stone
*Llethr*, slope
*Llithrig*, slippery
*Llyn, lake*
*Maen*, stone (maen hir, long stone or standing stone, i.e. menhir)
*Mawr (Fawr)*, big
*Moel (Foel)*, bare, rounded hill
*Mynydd (Fynydd)*, mountain
*Nant*, stream, brook
*Newydd,* new
*Ogof*, cave
*Pant*, small hollow
*Pen*, peak
*Pistyll*, waterfall, usually a water spout
*Pont (Bont)*, bridge
*Porth*, gate
*Pwll*, pool
*Rhaeadr*, waterfall
*Rhyd*, ford
*Saeth*, arrow
*Sarn*, causeway
*Sych*, dry
*Tref*, town
*Twll*, hole
*Ty*, house
*Uchaf*, highest
*Waun*, moor
*Wen*, white
*Y(Yr)*, the, of the
*Ynys*, island
*Ysgol*, ladder

MAPS AND MAPPING

Southern Wales is covered by a large number of Ordnance Survey 1:50,000 Landranger Sheets; it is unnecessary to list them all as not all of them are required by walks in the book. Those maps that are required are given at the beginning of each walk.

The Brecon Beacons National Park is covered by the 1:25,000 Outdoor Leisure Maps:

11    Central Area
12    Western Area
13    Eastern Area

In addition to which the lower Wye Valley and the Forest of Dean are covered by a fourth Outdoor Leisure Map:

14    Wye Valley and Forest of Dean

For those walks that are not covered by these larger scale maps, the information on each walk specifies the relevant 1:25 000 Pathfinder sheet that does cover it.

The maps given for each walk use conventional map signs, with the addition of the following:

| | |
|---|---|
| intact wall | gate |
| broken wall | kissing gate |
| fence or hedge | ladder stile |
| stile | indistinct path |
| distinct path | start point |
| no path | feature of interest |

Each map has a scale bar. They are drawn from personal observations, and so are not guaranteed to be absolutely to scale. Every effort has been made to ensure accuracy, but from time to time fences are erected or, more unusually, taken down. The author would be grateful for any information on such changes so that the book can be kept up to date.

MOUNTAIN SAFETY AND THE COUNTRY CODE

In comparison with the mountains of North Wales where the closeness of the Irish Sea increases the rate of fall of temperature with altitude and also enhances local winds, the hill ranges of South Wales, i.e. of the Brecon Beacons National Park, appear benign. True there is the same chilling effect with altitude, but it is less pronounced – about 1°C/150 metres (2°F/500 ft) – and the change in altitude is less. Nevertheless, to a wet, cold and lost walker these hills are real enough and the walker must be prepared for harsh conditions, particularly if he is on the hills in winter.

These comments are not made to make the hills seem a playground for supermen, or to dissuade anyone from walking on them. It is just that it would be irresponsible not to warn any newcomer to mountain areas of the tricks they can play. Be prepared: if you have not done so already, get a copy of *Safety on Mountains*, a very small booklet from the British Mountaineering Council that tackles the very large subject of individual responsibility and safety.

It is also important that anyone contemplating expeditions into mountainous areas should be able to use a map and compass. If you are not familiar with these critical items, you could do no better than obtain a copy of Kevin Walker's *Mountain Navigation Techniques*, published in the same Constable series as this guide.

The majority of the walks in the book follow distinct paths. Please keep to them. The National Parks' only real pollution problem is people, and the cars that bring them. Under the sort of traffic some of the hills receive the laid pavements in towns would groan after a few months. So, if on any of the walks the path is diverted to allow the ground to recover, of if there is a section of constructed pathway, be sympathetic to the problems. Of course it would be better if there were no obvious, scarring paths, but the only really successful method of reducing wear to zero would be to ban all walkers.

*The Country Code*

The Code was prepared by the Countryside Commission with the help and advice of the many organisations concerned with the welfare of the countryside.

Enjoy the country and respect its life and work.

Guard against all risk of fire.

Fasten all gates.

Keep dogs under close control.

Keep to public footpaths across all farmland.

Use gates and stiles to cross field boundaries.

Leave all livestock, machinery and crops alone.

Take your litter home.

Help to keep all water clean.

Protect wildlife, plants and trees.

Make no unnecessary noise.

# Setting the Scene

About 4 km (2$\frac{1}{2}$ miles) south-east from the Gower headland overlooking Worm's Head, near to Rhosili and to Walk 13 of this book, is a cave in the limestone cliff, reachable only at low tide. The cave, known as Paviland Cave, was investigated in the first quarter of the nineteenth century by William Buckland, Oxford geologist and Dean of Westminster. He found a collection of animal bones – hyena, cave bear, woolly rhinoceros, mammoth – together with some primitive stone tools, some ivory rods and rings, pierced shells and the headless skeleton of a human being stained red by ochre. As a creationist the good Dean was much exercised by his find: here was a recognisable human sharing a cave site with animals that pre-dated Archbishop Ussher's creation date of the evening of 22 October 4004 BC. The perplexed Dean decided – though whether he decided with the full vigour of intellectual honesty will never be known – that the burial was a later, Romano-British, addition to the cave. Since the skeleton was tiny he concluded it was that of a women, the Red Lady of Paviland.

Now we know that the skeleton was of a palaeolithic, Old Stone Age, man: when he lived, perhaps 20,000 years ago, the cave would have been further from the sea, the water level having risen several feet. Why the man was headless, and why the bones had been stained with ochre, is not known, though it is speculated that there was a ritual reason, similar burials having been found elsewhere in Europe.

The Red Lady is the best palaeolithic discovery so far in Wales, though that at King Arthur's Cave, near the River Wye and Walk 34, rivals it. For the next 15,000 years, until the palaeolithic hunters and their mesolithic, Middle Stone Age, successors were replaced by agriculturally proficient neolithic, New Stone Age, men, there are few remains. The neolithic people were the first to leave a tangible sign of their existence on the landscape, for these were the cromlech builders. Cromlechs – the name is actually Welsh and is the now generally accepted word for structures also called quoits or dolmens – are burial chambers. They consist of a number of upright stones supporting a large flat roofing slab. In their original form the chambers would have been earthed over to create a long barrow, but in many instances the earth has long since weathered away to leave the uprights and cap stones, gaunt and hugely impressive against the sky.

There are several fine examples of cromlechs in southern Wales. Near Cardiff, the Tinkinswood long barrow is more or less complete, its earth mound held in place by dry-stone walling virtually indistinguishable from that which would be produced by a modern waller. Also near Cardiff, the St Lythans cromlech consists of three uprights and a single cap stone. On the Gower Peninsula, Maen Ceti, or Arthur's Stone, has a 25-ton cap stone supported by nine uprights. The name Arthur's Stone derives from a legend that Arthur was one day walking near Carmarthen, when he found a stone in his shoe. Angrily snatching it out he flung it away – to this lonely spot on Gower. In one tale, therefore, we see the Celtic love of a superhuman hero, and recognise the awe that the cromlechs held for later inhabitants of an area. Who but a giant could raise a 25-ton stone into the air?

The best cromlech in our area is, without doubt, Pentre Ifan on the northern flank of the Preseli Hills. Here a 17-ton cap stone is supported by four uprights that taper, almost to points. The effect is, therefore, of the fingers of a hand pointing upwards to support the cap. In its original form the cromlech was covered by a mound 36 m (120 ft) long, a mound that would have had a walled forecourt as at Tinkinswood.

The neolithic cromlech builders were replaced by, or evolved into, Bronze Age people who buried their dead in round barrows or cairns, and are widely believed to be responsible for the erection of menhirs – single standing stones, the word deriving from the Welsh, *maen hir* , long stone – and stone circles. The most prolific barrow remains are to be found on the Preseli Hills, and there are a large number of single stones scattered throughout southern Wales. Stone circles are far less numerous, and those that do exist are considerably less imposing than, say, Avebury. One good site, Cerrig Duon, is visited on Walk 17. This absence of stone circles is especially ironic since it has now been proven that some of the stones for Stonehenge were quarried from the eastern end of the Preseli Hills, probably by the Beaker Folk, themselves a Bronze Age people. The quarry site is visited by Walk 11, the Notes for that Walk exploring in greater depth the Stonehenge connection. Walk 4 visits an impressive menhir, Maen Serth, steeped in legend.

Following the Bronze Age Wales saw an influx of the people with whom the country is now synonymous, the Celts. That name was not used by the Iron Age folk themselves, but derives from the Roman Keltoi, a word interchangeable with Galli, for the people who lived in Gaul or France. The Romans saw these Celts as barbaric savages, forever boasting about their own and their leaders' abilities in battles, and with a priesthood – the Druids – who were pagan mumbo-jumboists and wielded a frightening power. In reality the Celts were a cultured, civilised people, if a little warlike, whose bards – the singers of praises – compensated for the lack of a written language, and whose Druid priests practised an earth-magic no better, but certainly no worse, than that of many other ancient cults. There is evidence from the magnificent hoard of sickles, razors, fittings and so on found in 1912 in Llyn Fawr in Glamorgan, which contained both bronze and iron implements, that the Celts did not annihilate their Bronze Age predecessors. Indeed if the legend of the Lady of the Lake is a folk story then the transition from one age to the next was one of painless assimilation, a triumph for the 'barbaric' Celts. The lake of the legend is visited by Walk 16, a Note to that Walk detailing the story and its potential implications.

The most tangible reminder of the Iron Age Celts is their hill forts, defensible settlements or retreats, which are dotted all over southern Britain. Maiden Castle in Dorset is undoubtedly the best British hill fort, Tre'r Ceiri on the Lleyn Peninsula is the best in Wales, but several of our Walks visit or go close to good sites. Walk 10 passes a promontory fort, one built on a headland and so protected on several sides by sheer cliffs, while Walk 26 visits a more conventional hill fort.

The Romans subdued the Celts in Britain with a combination of the short sword and the seductive influence of the Roman lifestyle. They were at pains to end Druidism, invading and destroying the priesthood's island sanctuary, Anglesey, a desecration that was, in part, responsible for the uprising of Boudicca. But at first the Roman advance in Wales was resisted. One notable leader was Caratacus who rallied the Silurians and Ordovices, tribes of Wales, and fought a brave and prolonged campaign. Walk 34 visits one site that has been proposed as an important one in the campaign, which ended, in AD51, with the betrayal and capture of Caratacus. So well had he fought and so impressed were the Romans with his demeanour in captivity that his life was spared and he lived in honoured and prosperous exile in Rome. To assist in the holding of Wales the Romans built many forts connected by roads to the massive legionary fortresses at Deva, Chester, and Isca, Carleon. The latter, to the north-east of Newport, is one of the finest Roman sites in Britain, a close rival being the market town of Venta Silurium at Caerwent a few miles to the east. Neither of these sites is on one of our Walks, but Walk 7 does visit the Roman gold mines of Dolaucothi.

Following the departure of the Romans Britain fell to the Saxons, who landed in the east and gradually pushed westward, cutting the Celts of Wales off from those of Cornwall at the battle of Dyrham in 577. Prior to that their advance had been halted, if only for a decade or so, by a mysterious Celtic leader called Arthur, a king who is now woven into the fabric of Welsh mythology. Arthur is found in many tales from the *Mabinogion* ; there are stones and other features without number named for him; lakes abound that hold Excalibur beneath their surfaces and secret caves where he sleeps awaiting the call to return to save his people can be found in several counties. But the tales were told by a people deprived of their country, for the Saxons took Britain right up to the borders of what is now Wales. They even named the people – these were the Wallas , the foreigners, the name also giving us Valais in Switzerland and Walloon in Belgium. The Celts, by contrast, referred to themselves as Cymry, fellow countrymen, and to their country as Cymru.

The Saxon invasion of Britain showed a flaw in the Celtic tribal system that not only cost them dear then, but was to do so again and again. The Celts were very good at forming small groups and fighting amongst themselves. This inter-tribal battling was 'helped' by the system of inheritance: when a chief died his lands were divided among his sons who, if they did not fight among themselves, were usually invaded by neighbours made effectively stronger by the reduction in size of the chieftainship. Even when faced by a common enemy – Saxon, Norman or English – the Welsh could never unite for long enough to gain independence. Behind Offa's Dyke, built in the late eighth century by a Saxon king of Mercia, and followed, in part, by Walk 36, the Welsh formed and reformed small kingdoms.

Rhodri Mawr is generally named the first king, or Prince, of Wales, but though he ruled the old kingdoms – now new counties or districts – of Gwynedd, Powys and Ceredigion (Cardiganshire), he did not rule Gwent, Morgannwg (Glamorgan), Dyfed or Brycheiniog (Breconshire). A later king, Hywel Dda, Hywel the Good, whose fort may be visited on Walk 27, is also mentioned as a Prince of all Wales, though he, too, ruled only the larger part of the country. Gruffydd ap Llywelyn – Gruffydd, the son of Llywelyn – did unite the country, in 1041, but he soon overreached himself by trying to expand eastward across the dyke. Edward the Confessor sent Earl Harold Godwinson, later to be king and to die at Hastings, to deal with the usurper. Gruffydd was killed and Wales subdued.

Soon there was a new enemy, the Normans who defeated the Saxons and established along the old border a group of 'buffer states' to protect England from the Welsh. These states were the Marcher lordships, 'march' here having its original meaning of boundary. The Marcher lords were allowed to take as much of Wales as they felt they could hold, a right that, not surprisingly, brought them into constant conflict with the Welsh. Some parts of Wales, chiefly the mountainous backbone and north, the Normans left largely untouched, but the more fertile, less hostile south they did take. Here, too, they installed a colony of Flemings from Holland and Belgium. Quite why this happened is not known: some maintain that the Flemish settlements were tolerated rather than encouraged, the Flemings themselves fleeing the flooding of their own lands – at that time also under Norman domination. Others see the settlements in more political or economic terms, as deliberate actions to form a buffer, or to bring much needed agricultural or mercantile skills to a backward area. Whatever the reasons, the Flemings of Pembrokeshire and Gower were to prove a disastrous group to Welsh princes, most notably at the time of the Glyndwr rebellion.

Llywelyn ap Iorwerth, known now as Llywelyn the Great, succeeded to Gwynedd in 1203 and soon added Powys and some land in South Wales to his kingdom. He took advantage of the times, for the barons of England were combining to stand up to King John, Llywelyn's father-in-law. By siding with the barons Llywelyn was able to gain significant rights for Wales in Magna Carta, and by the time of his death in 1240 the country, while not united – the Fleming colony of the south being decidedly opposed to Welsh unity – had an air of independence. Llywelyn's death caused the usual fragmentation, though his grandson, Llywelyn ap Gruffydd (Llywelyn the Last) fought again for unity. He was made Prince of Wales by Henry III under the terms of the Treaty of Montgomery in 1267, but Henry's successor, Edward I, was a stronger adversary. Edward reduced Llywelyn's position to that of a baron at the Treaty of Aberconwy in 1277, a move not guaranteed to win the Welshman's heart. Llywelyn rose in rebellion again in 1282 and was killed in a minor skirmish near Builth Wells. Walk 33 lies close to the place of death of the last Welsh Prince of Wales.

Following Llywelyn's death Edward I decided that never again would he be troubled by the Welsh, and he erected his 'Ring of Stone' castles to ensure they could not rebel again: Conwy, to secure the river crossing into Gwynedd; Caernarfon to ensure that the mountains of Gwynedd could not be used as a barrier; Beaumaris to secure Anglesey, the Granary of Wales, and others. These castles are in North Wales, traditional seat of opposition. Our Walks do not visit any Edwardian castles, but Walk 14 does visit Carreg Cennen, an impressive castle from earlier times in the Welsh-Norman struggle.

In the wars of Edward III the Welsh fought with distinction at Crécy and Poitiers for their English king, but the Marcher lords continued to treat their Welsh subjects with contempt, over-taxing them and using them as serfs. Finally, in 1400, following yet another clash between a Norman Marcher lord and a Welsh neighbour, there was another rebellion. Owain Glyndwr was a strange man to lead a revolt: perhaps fifty years old, a sophisticated, educated, multi-lingual man with a distinguished record in the English king's court and army. But lead one he did, a savage ten-year rebellion that left Wales and the Welsh exhausted and starved. Walk 2 visits the scene of Glyndwr's first victory – over the Flemings of South Wales – while Walk 3 follows a section of a footpath named for the leader. Other walks recall events in the rebellion so far-reaching was it and so long did it last. Finally the Welsh wanted peace at any price and despite savage legislation enacted against them they still fought bravely for Henry V at Agincourt. In the Wars of the Roses that followed the Welsh were split. Even after the half-Welsh

Henry Tudor landed in Pembrokeshire in 1485 and wrested the crown from Richard III at Bosworth there were some Welshmen who saw not a Welsh king but a usurper.

Henry VIII unified England and Wales, a unification that gave political rights but still allowed the Welsh to be exploited by their English neighbours. When the mineral wealth of Wales became apparent it was chiefly the Welsh who did the work, the English who took the profit. Never was this more true than in the northern slate quarries: the metal mines of mid-Wales, fine examples of which are visited by Walks 3 and 5(a), were not quite rich enough for serious long-term exploitation.

In the south the minerals were coal and iron. Both are ancient industries, dating at least from the Roman occupation, but real exploitation came only a couple of hundred years ago. The Welsh ironstone band stretched from Blaenafon to Hirwaun, about 30 km (18 miles), and produced good ore with up to 40 per cent of iron. The iron was extracted in charcoal-fed forges, huge areas of forest in the lower valleys being cleared to make the fuel. Since 16 tons of wood were required to produce 1 ton of iron, the industry (or forest) was only saved by the discovery of coking coal. Coal itself had been recognised as a fuel at least by Roman times. Early mining was by means of the bell-pit. A vertical shaft was sunk until the coal seam was hit and from its base men would then work outwards into the seam, producing a hand-bell-like structure. This was hard and dangerous work: coal and men had to be hand-winched up the shaft, and since there would be many pits the horizontal digging had every chance of producing an unstable, and collapsing, roof.

Later, when shafts and digs were longer, gas rather than collapse was the major hazard, and elaborate systems for drawing air into the mine were devised. Only the introduction of the Davy lamp made working really safe: as late as 1860 over a hundred men and boys were killed in an explosion in a South Wales pit. The harsh and dangerous working conditions, poor housing and even poorer living conditions developed a strong sense of community among the miners, many of whom were not Welsh but had been brought in as cheap labour from the Midlands. The mine-owners included some colourful characters – David Davies, whose statue now dominates his native village of Llandinam near Llanidloes, was down to his last half-crown after he had paid his men, and gave that to them as well. Impressed, they gave him one last shift, and discovered the Rhondda seams, or so the story goes – but most were grey men more interested in profit than social welfare. Unionism was strongly opposed: at one gathering at Merthyr the commander of the troops called to quell and disperse the 'riot' had one of his men slice a dog in half with his sword as an example to the crowd of what could happen. The displeasure over working conditions became a more general grievance over social conditions and led to the Chartist movement, dealt with in the Note to Walk 23 which visits an important site in the movement's history. It also led to the rise in popularity of Nonconformist churches, the famous Valley Chapels. The established Church invariably sided with the Establishment – the mine owners – the miners seeking solace in the new faiths which practised a more Christian form of Christianity.

Gradually things improved and the area became one of the mainstays of British industry. As elsewhere however there has now been a general decline, the iron and steel works are gone, the pits are closing. Nowhere is this, or the history of both industries, better shown than at Blaenafon, the centre for Walk 32. At Blaenafon the pit-head baths have not become a supermarket, as Max Boyce's lament for a lost way of life maintains, but part of a Heritage Museum

# Plynlimon

In the middle of the nineteenth century W. F. Peacock, the traveller, wrote of his trip to Plynlimon. He encountered 'bogland; uncertain sponge, with black pitchy water ... dark herbage thrives and its complexion is just about as ghostly and healthless as you can imagine'. Peacock's boots had an undeniably black baptism. He was lucky, he said, to escape from a hellish prison where a man climbing alone was 'little better than a fool. He has one chance of returning in safety; he has ninety-nine chances of being seen no more in life'.

Since then – and perhaps before – Plynlimon has had a bad press. It is 'a sodden weariness'. Even Thomas Pennant, a self-confident traveller, was 'dissuaded from making it a visit, being informed that it was an uninteresting object, the base most extensive, the top boggy and the view over a dreary and almost uninhabited country'. As a complete contrast, it is widely believed that Coleridge thought of the line 'Water, water, everywhere. Nor any drop to drink' while on Plynlimon when he and a companion were parched with thirst during a walk across it.

Both suggestions about the range are justified, but not widely justified. It is certainly true that Plynlimon has boggy sections: the extensive peat bogs near Blaenhafren can be an 'interesting' place to be after heavy rain, and much of the upland plateau shows frequent outcrops of bog moss. And, given a few days of dry weather, the mosses dry out dramatically, to the point where they scrunch under foot, and the Mother of Rivers can then be fairly discreet about where exactly her rivers are.

Plynlimon has long been considered one of the three mountains of Wales – along with Snowdon and Cadair Idris – and is indeed of the same rock. The underlying rock is Ordovician, set among the Silurian rock like a displaced section of Snowdonia. But there is none of the rugged grandeur of the Snowdon peaks, the best Plynlimon can offer being the broken cliffs above the Rheidol's source, Llyn Llygad Rheidol. Rather, the hills here resemble the green humps of the Carneddau. It is said that when the famous Alpine guide Jean Charlet came here he gaped at the hills and claimed that God had forgotten to put tops on them. This roundness, the lowness of the hills – Pen Pumlumon Fawr does not quite make 2500 ft – and its reputation, mean that Plynlimon stays quiet when the more northerly hills are groaning under the weight of travellers. That is what I mean by having a bad press: in reality Plynlimon has much to offer: spectacular views – on a good day virtually every other mountain range in Wales can be seen – fine valleys, well set lakes, and a wealth of Celtic history and folk lore.

Conventional wisdom holds that Pen Pumlumon Fawr should be climbed from the south, from Eisteddfa Gurig, but that route commits the walker to a long ascent with limited views and few other redeeming features. We go north instead, choosing an ascent line that allows views northward to Snowdonia and of the reservoir lakes of Nant-y-moch and Llyn Llygad Rheidol. An easier walk visits the lonely Hyddgen valley, scene of a desperate battle, while a third visits the even more frequently neglected eastern side of the range.

## Walk 1 Pen Pumlumon Fawr

Our first route climbs to the highest point of the Plynlimon area. Here, however, we climb from the north. The route is a little shorter than that from Eisteddfa Gurig, but involves about 100 m (330 ft) of extra climbing. To compensate it offers ever-better outlooks including a view of a finely set mountain lake.

*Walk category* : Difficult ($3^1/_2$ hours or $5^1/_2$ hours with extension).

*Length* : 10 km (6 miles) [+ 7 km ($4^1/_2$ miles) for extension].

*Ascent* : 400 m (1300 ft) [+ 100 m (330 ft) for extension].

*Maps* :  Landranger Sheet 135; Pathfinder Sheet 927 (SN 68/78) Tal-y-bont and Ponterwyd; and 1:25,000 First Series SN 88 Pumlumon-Arwystli.

*Starting and finishing point* : At 768 875 beside the road on the southern edge of the Nant-y-moch reservoir. This road is reached by turning right off the mountain road from Ponterwyd to Tal-y-bont just before the reservoir dam is reached.

WALKS 1 & 2 PLYNLIMON

N

AFON HYDDGEN

GLYNDWR COVENANT STONES 2(1)

G   S

FOOTBR

NANT

FAINC DDU

500m

MAESNANT CENTRE

S2   G

G

LLYN LLYGAD RHEIDOL 1(1)

G

550m   600m

S1

NANT-Y-MOCH RESERVOIR

350m   400m   450m   500m

PUMLUMON FACH

½   1Km

½m.

PONTERWYD

AFON HENGWM

SOURCE OF RIVER SEVERN 1(3)

600m

650m

PEN PUMLUMON - ARWYSTLI

550m
600m
650m
700m
650m
700m

GRAIG LAS

650m

SOURCE OF RIVER WYE 1(3)

700m

m
PEN PUMLUMON FAWR
- 752m    1(2)

From the metalled road a rough track rises steeply towards Llyn Llygad Rheidol (see note (1)). At a gate go through, then leave the track to go east and upwards towards the obvious summit. Trend leftward to the stream of Maesnant whose slight valley can be followed to below the twin knobby summits of Pumlumon Fach. From the slightly higher – the more easterly – knob there is a fine view of Llyn Llygad Rheidol (see (1) Llyn Llygad Rheidol). From the knob the summit of Pumlumon Fawr can no longer be seen, but it quickly emerges again when the ridge to the south is climbed (see (2) Pen Pumlumon Fawr).

In the 'old days' not so many years ago – the plateau-ridge to the east was free access land and a very fine walk could be made by way of the source of the Wye (see (3) River sources), the subsidiary summit of Pen Pumlumon-Arwystli and the source of the Severn. From there a descent route going slightly north of west reached the Hengwm valley which was followed to join Route 2. Of late a huge new fence has been constructed along the ridge, a fence that descends northward and southward, cutting off access to both the ridge and the Wye source. There are no gates or stiles, though in fairness it must be said that there is also no right of way. It is very sad. Of course the route can still be followed by the careful and cautious, but it does involve the crossing of private land.

The 'official' route follows the fence eastward in order to traverse the steep cliffs above the lake, following the eastern edge of the cwm southward to a point where a descent can be made to the outflow of the lake. From there a route can be made down the right bank of the Nant-y-Llyn to reach Route 2. This is not a good walk with little to compensate for the poor going. Better to follow the track back to the start passing an interesting collection of small pools set on a rocky plateau.

(1) *Llyn Llygad Rheidol*
Perhaps as little as 10,000 years ago an ice sheet covered the summit plateau of Plynlimon , the ice flowing out in all directions. Northward the ice scoured a hollow, over-deepening it so that when the ice melted a lake was formed behind a dam of deposited glacial moraine. Llyn

The Nant-y-moch reservoir from Pen Pumlumon Fawr

Llygad Rheidol is an excellent example of such a glacially formed lake and is beautifully set below the broken cliffs of Graig Las. Today the lake is a reservoir, as the notice with the dire threats tells the visitor, with an artificial outflow, the water directed down an ugly, but easily crossed, concrete channel.

(2) *Pen Pumlumon Fawr*

The *Mabinogion*, that fountain head of Celtic folklore, tells of the Arthurian knights Kay and Bedevere sitting on this summit in 'the greatest wind in the world'. Certainly the summit's position and its height – low by Snowdonian standards, but high in relation to the surrounding land – do appear to attract the wind, and there are many who have been grateful to crouch in the low-walled summit shelter. The hill's name is usually given as deriving from *pump*, Welsh for five, and 'an ancient word for...'. The latter is sometimes river, sometimes peak and never convincing. Certainly it is possible to distinguish five tops, but equally easy to see three or seven. The Rheidol, Wye and Severn rise here, as do many other rivers – the area is a significant watershed and the mother of rivers – but it is certainly difficult to claim an especially noteworthy group of five.

In 1401 Owain Glyndwr raised his standard on Plynlimon, a monument near the eastern end of the Nant-y-moch dam noting the event. There followed the battle of Hyddgen, detailed in Note (1) of Route 2. Now the Welsh for a standard is *llumon*, which looks suspiciously like the 'limon' of Plynlimon and the 'lumon' of Pumlumon. Is Pumlumon really Pen Llumon, the Hill of the Standard?

(3) *River sources*

Though they are geographically close – the Wye and Severn are born about 4 km ($2^1/_2$ miles) apart – the two river sources could hardly be more different. The Wye starts boldly, within yards it is flowing in a well defined valley, while the Severn has no definable start, rising tentatively amid the peat bogs that make up the land between Pen Pumlumon Arwystli and Cumbiga. The names reverse the process. 'Wye' is probably Celtic and probably means rapid, though little is definite. 'Severn' derives from Hafren. In Celtic legend Locrinus, the King of Britain, was married to Gwendolen, daughter of the King of Cornwall. Sadly Locrinus loved Estrildis and a daughter, Hafren, was born. Ultimately Locrinus left Gwendolen to live with Estrildis and Hafren. Outraged, Gwendolen travelled to Cornwall, raised an army and returned to wreak vengeance. Locrinus was killed in battle, and Estrildis and Hafren were bound and thrown into a nearby river. As they drowned Gwendolen realised that she should not have murdered the child as Hafren was innocent of any crime. Attempts to save the child failed, and the remorseful Gwendolen named the river in her memory. In Welsh the river is still Hafren, the source being named Blaenhafren. The English form derives from the Roman, whose aspirant was 's' not 'h' and who therefore called the river Sabrina.

The land between the two rivers is known as Fferllys, and is the home of the Tylwyth Teg, the fairyfolk. On this land the ferns (of which there are not many) bear a small blue flower on St John's Eve. If the seeds of the flowers are gathered in white cloth – no hand must touch them – the gatherer will become invisible so that he/she may enter a lover's room undetected. Alternatively, if you stay in Fferllys an elf will exchange your seeds for a purse of gold.

## Walk 2 The Hyddgen Valley

This short walk visits the site of Owain Glyndwr's first success in battle. It is a good introduction to the joys of Plynlimon.

*Walk category* : Easy ($1^1/_2$ hours).

*Length* : 6 km (4 miles).

*Ascent* : 50 m (150 ft).

*Maps* : Landranger Sheet 135; Pathfinder Sheet 927 (SN 68/78) Tal-y-bont and Ponterwyd.

*Starting and finishing point* : Beside the road, as for Walk 1, but closer to the road end near the Maesnant Outdoor Pursuits Centre.

Go through the gate to the right of the gate for the Outdoor Centre to reach a stony track. Follow this through another gate and on to a ruined building, left. To the right along the track the steep ground of Fainc Ddu Uchaf and Fainc Ddu Isaf offers fine views. A little way beyond the ruin the track bears left to the river Hengwm which can be forded to a gate. Alternatively a path leads on past old walls to reach a footbridge with a stile beyond. Either way the Hyddgen valley is reached, up which a path leads over peaty ground. Sadly the Cerrig Cyfamod Glyndwr (see (1) Glyndwr Covenant Stones) are across the Afon Hyddgen and protected by a fence, but the walker can see them plainly. To return, the outward route is reversed. From the bridge a small waterfall in the Hengwm valley can be reached by following the river upstream (eastwards). The going is a little arduous however, and many will settle for the trip back with its expanding view over the Nant-y-moch reservoir.

## (1) *Glyndwr Covenant Stones*

Following the Norman invasion of England the Norman kings left Wales to itself, content to place a barrier between themselves and the Welsh, their impenetrable mountains and vile weather. The barrier was human, the Marcher lords. These lords owned the land on the march, or border and the western boundary of their estates was undefined. In Wales they could take all the land they thought they could hold. Not surprisingly this, together with the frequent passing of anti-Welsh legislation, left Wales with a seething undercurrent of resentment. Often there were uprisings, some of them major as with the problems in the late thirteenth century that led to the building of the 'Ring of Stone' castles.

In 1399 Henry Bolingbroke added to the bitterness by usurping the crown – as many Welshmen saw it – from Richard II. Then in 1400 the new Henry IV supported Lord Grey of Ruthin against Owain Glyndwr, a high-born Welshman whose home was at Sycharth on the flank of the Berwyns. Owain was forced to flee Grey and with a band of men rode to loot the towns of Ruthin, Denbigh and Flint. Henry arrived with an army, the countryside quietened and Glyndwr disappeared. He came here, to the Hyddgen valley, where, in 1401, he was joined by a small group of men, perhaps 400 in all. News of this 'army' spread to South Wales where a group of pro-English, Flemish wool-trade settlers decided

The Hyddgen valley

to act swiftly to protect their interests. An armed band was formed and marched north.

Glyndwr was still new to rebellion and his men took none of the precautions necessary to protect themselves. Consequently the Flemish army managed to reach Plynlimon not only unmolested, but also unseen. And not only to reach Plynlimon, but to reach the ridge above the Hyddgen valley – bear in mind that in 1401 there was no Nant-y-moch reservoir. From the high ground they powered in on the Glyndwr men whom they outnumbered perhaps as many as five to one. With retreat impossible and defeat and death probable, the Welsh fought like tigers, stemming, then turning the Flemish flow. Against all odds Glyndwr was victorious, the Flemish army fleeing in confusion leaving behind hundreds of dead.

News of the victory turned a local uprising into a full scale rebellion as the Welsh rallied to their new leader. Today the only sign of the battle in this peaceful valley are the two dazzling white calcite blocks that the Welsh hauled here to commemorate their victory and to pledge their support for Glyndwr.

## Walk 3 Owain Glyndwr's Way

This walk follows a section of Owain Glyndwr's Way, a long-distance footpath waymarked by Powys County Council from Knighton to Welshpool, by way of Machynlleth. Owain Glyndwr, a prince of Powys, is mentioned in Note (1) of Walk 2. Our route follows only a three-mile section of the fine 125-mile walk, deflecting from it to view the ruins of the mines that made Dylife, the starting village, important over a century ago.

*Walk category* : Intermediate ($3^1/_2$ hours)

*Length* : 13 km (8 miles).

*Ascent* : 300 m (1000 ft).

Plynlimon from the Glyndwr Covenant Stones

*Maps* : Landranger Sheet 135 (Aberystwyth and surrounding area);
        1:25,000 First Series SN 89 (Staylittle).

*Starting and finishing point* : At the lay-by beside the road opposite the
Star Inn, Dylife. The village is reached along a narrow mountain road
that leaves the B4518 just north of Staylittle and emerges at Machynlleth
by way of the town golf course.

From the lay-by take the signed track that rises steeply and to the left up
the hillside southward. At a gate go through, leaving the track by turning
half-right for a gate and stile. Go through or over and follow the rutted
path beyond over the summit of Penycrocbren (see (1) Penycrocbren).
At the summit there is another gate and stile pair beyond which the path
reaches a third pair. Go through or over again and down to a track,
passing yet a fourth gate and stile pair. Here Glyndwr's Way goes right,
but we go left along the track. Go through a gate and follow the track as
it bends left. Technically the route goes right here, following the right of
way around the hill westward. A fence has been built across the way
with no stile and this necessitates a steep descent to the Afon Clywedog
reached just west of the old mines (see (2) Dyfngwm Mine). At the river
a half-stile allows progress westward. The Twymyn can be followed
upstream making use of a steep track which crosses a slope that is never
easy and occasionally desperate. It is a most beautiful stream and enters
a narrow, rocky gorge that is even more spectacular. To the right there
are old water-filled shafts, the rock near them having been worked into
weird shapes. There is even one keyhole through the rock.
    Further progress upstream is halted by the gorge and although an
escape can be made up the right side – follow what remains of a fence –
it is a steep, loose and very difficult climb. It is better to retrace, going
up the steep slope to the top of the gorge as soon as possible. A definite,
though sometimes indistinct, path is reached and followed leftward over
a half-stile and then down to a footbridge and the Nant Goch, a tributary
of the Clywedog.
    The bridge is not for the faint-hearted, being only two well-spaced
girders for half its length and having a handrail that seems to need, rather
than lend, support. Beyond, the path continues to farm buildings and a

more straightforward track. Bear right where this joins another, continuing past Glaslyn (see (3) Glaslyn) to a large 'lay-by' on the left. Here we rejoin Glyndwr's Way, but now going west-east. Go left on a grassy, rutted path and follow it to the summit of Foel Fadian (see (4) Foel Fadian). A fence on Foel Fadian's eastern flank requires a descent of the ascent path back to the track. Go left and follow the track to a minor road. Go right taking the road verge back to Dylife (see (5) Dylife). At a farm track Glyndwr's Way goes right, but this entails a recrossing of Penycrocbren.

(1) *Penycrocbren*
This hill, 466 m (1530 ft) high, is the 'Hill of the Gallows', so called from a supposedly legendary story told of the time when Dylife was an important mining town. The town's only blacksmith, Siôn y Gof (John the Smith), believed that his wife was being unfaithful to him and decided to murder her. As the couple had a young daughter, Siôn knew that his wife's lone disappearance would cause suspicions, and so he killed his daughter as well, throwing the bodies into a disused mine shaft. He told the villagers that the pair had left him, but later, by accident or by search after doubts had been raised, the bodies were found. Siôn was tried, convicted and sentenced to hang. At the time the bodies of the hanged were left to rot on gibbets as a warning, and it was decided that Siôn should lie in a full iron cage, his head in a smaller cage. As the only local smith Siôn was therefore set to work to make the cage. Whether this was a calculated act of vengeance is unclear, but Siôn made his cage, was hanged on the Hill of Gallows and gibbeted inside his own handiwork. So the legend goes.

In 1938 two men digging on the hill uncovered the cage, proving that the story was not legend but fact. Today the skull of Siôn y Gof, still in its iron cage, is displayed in St Fagan's Museum near Cardiff. No civilised person can find great sympathy with a man who killed not only his wife but his own, and innocent, child, but it is difficult to view the skull without feeling a little pity for a man set such an appalling task.

Centuries before Siôn's hanging Penycrocbren – then, presumably, bearing another name – was the site of a small Roman fort, as a Roman military road traversed the northern flank of Plynlimon, on the way to

FOEL
FADIAN
(565m)
④

550m

▲

500m

MACHYNLLETH

50

450m

GLASLYN
③

500m

450m  NANT GOCH  450m

S

FARM

FOOTBRIDGE

N

400m

⑤ DYLIFE  STAR INN

350m

FFRWD FAWR

PENYCROCBREN.

450m. ①

400m

STAYLITTLE

S  G

G  G  G

S

450m

G

DYFNGWM MINE. ②

450m

400m

AFON CLYWEDOG

½  1 Km.

½ m

Machynlleth and the Dyfi river. Today it takes an expert to discern the lines of the old walls.

## (2) *Dyfngwm Mine*

The Dyfngwm Mine was only part of the Dylife mines, one of the foremost mines of Wales. It was widely believed that it was a very rich lead mine, but its history – over a very short lifetime of around thirty years – was one of mismanagement and poor commercial sense. The mine closed in 1867, but was reopened in the early years of this century, though with little more success. The returns from the mine show that in addition to lead it produced copper and a little zinc.

The Dylife mines themselves, closer to the Star Inn and soon to be turned into an Industrial Archaeological Trail, were probably worked in Roman times. Here too the ore yielded lead and copper and at the height of its prosperity the mine employed over 300 people, with the now ghostly Dylife village being a bustling place of over 1000 inhabitants. At the site was the biggest waterwheel ever erected in Wales, the 63 ft (19 m) Red Wheel. Today the wheel pit is a rubbish dump.

Those wishing to know more of the Dylife mines should consult Part 4 of David Bick's *The Old Metal Mines of Mid-Wales*.

## (3) *Glaslyn*

This fine lake is another blue-grey sheet of water bearing the name Glaslyn (blue-grey lake!). Unlike the Glaslyn that lies below Snowdon, reputed home of Excalibur and the *afanc*, this lake is merely bottomless. Glaslyn and its surrounding area, a piece of heather moor rare on Plynlimon, are a Site of Special Scientific Interest. Ducks, swans and goosanders winter here and the area is home to the peregrine and the merlin. Equally interesting is the plant life, which includes heath bedstraw, cowberry and ivy-leaved bellflower.

## (4) *Foel Fadian*

Foel Fadian, at 564 m (1850 ft), was the highest mountain in the old county of Montgomeryshire. It seems sad that the redrawing of county boundaries relegated this fine peak to being just another lowish hill in Powys. From the summit the views are superb. South is Plynlimon, a shapelier block than many give it credit for, while northward are the hills

Ruined tombstones at Dylife

of Snowdonia. Equally good is the view west, over the farmland of the southern side of the Dyfi valley, the river itself and Cardigan Bay. Foel Fadian offers what is arguably the best sunset viewpoint in this book.

## (5) *Dylife*

The Star Inn and the cemetery with its rusting ironwork and shattered gravestones seem to belie the fact that this village was once home to over 1000 people – a big village locally, even by the standards of the day. The village name derives from 'flood' or 'torrent', and it is generally believed that this is a reference to Ffrwd Fawr, the big stream, a spectacular waterfall a kilometre or so east of the village. At 45 m (150 ft) Ffrwd Fawr is one of the highest free-falling waterfalls in Wales and is extraordinary for the volume of water that falls, the Afon Twymyn that feeds it rising only about 4 km ($2^1/_2$ miles) from the head. Below the hard sandstone horseshoe of the falls the Twymyn turns sharply northward, flowing through a magnificent, almost textbook, glaciated valley.

The Clywedog valley

# Elenydd

South of Plynlimon is a high plateau of barren moorland deeply cut by
river valleys. To the west the plateau fails to reach the shore of Cardigan
Bay, falling gracefully to become the eastern side of the Teifi valley,
while to the south it extends as far as Llandovery. Eastward the
boundary is the valley road between Llandovery and Llandrindod Wells,
the hills of Mynydd Eppynt to the east of the main A483 being quite
different, but north of Llandrindod the situation is less clear. The plateau
there actually extends to the English border, though it is usually sub-
divided. To the east of Llandrindod is the Radnor Forest, while to the
north of the town is a lower, more cultivated landscape that is crossed by
Owain Glyndwr's Way. West of Llandrindod, indeed west of the Wye
valley that cuts decisively through the plateau, is the real Elenydd, a land
of uncompromising, barren moor, deeply dissected by valleys that have
been flooded to form reservoirs, the reservoirs of Claerwen and the Elan
valley. The flooding provided drinking water for the Midlands. The facts
about the dams, the surface area, volume of water, and daily flows are
staggering, but it is always an emotive point when wild land is deluged
to satisfy an English thirst. The loss of heritage can be severe. Here
Cwm Elan was lost, a house once occupied by the poet Shelley whose
eccentricities – including the sailing of boats made from five-pound
notes on the local stream – no doubt kept the locals in gossip for weeks.

   The name Elenydd I have stolen from Giraldus Cambrensis, Gerald of
Wales. This part-Norman, part-Welsh cleric was born – in the
magnificent castle of Manorbier in southern Pembrokeshire and near to
Walk 12 – in the mid-twelfth century and journeyed around Wales in
1188 with Archbishop Baldwin to gain support for the Third Crusade.
Gerald was an ambitious man who wanted to be Archbishop of St
David's. He was also outspoken and blessed with a gift for invective.
The latter traits were at odds with the former ambition and Gerald died
in obscurity in the early part of the thirteenth century. He would be
forgotten today, except perhaps by the persistent historian, were it not
for two books that he wrote on his Welsh travels. One, *The Journey
through Wales*, is a description of the Baldwin journey, the other, *The
Description of Wales*, is a geographical, socio-economic study. Each is

brilliant, the first having a chastening effect on all who write on travelling in Wales, being at once the first book written on the subject and (arguably) the best.

Gerald used the word Elenydd to differentiate the mountains of southern Wales from those of Eryri in North Wales. From this geography it is clear that he names the area as described above for which there is now no accepted name. It is widely assumed that the name derives from the Afon Elan, the flooding of whose valley yielded the Craig Goch, Penygarreg, Carreg-ddu and, in part, Caban-coch reservoirs. Tantalisingly, Gerald reveals that in 'English'the area was known as Moruge, a name that has not only become extinct, but defies explanation.

In its northern and central sections Elenydd is not a land to be trifled with, being devoid of real features and paths, with a vegetation that can make strong walkers weep and a lack of habitation that makes it feel remote and vaguely hostile. It is a place for the well-equipped and experienced walker to find peace and an inner challenge, but a difficult place to offer a Best Walk which both does justice to the area and does not place the walker in a potentially unfriendly position.

Our first walk makes use of a couple of well-defined ridges to explore some good views and a couple of interesting ancient sites. The second walk has two variations, one a fine river valley, the other a fascinating industrial archaeological site. The third walk takes a tour around some smaller lakes, visiting the real Elenydd in a controlled way.

## Walk 4 Penrhiw-Wen

Between the Elan valley reservoirs and the Wye valley the Elenydd plateau is partially split by a tumbling stream. This walk takes the ridges that define that stream's valley, ridges which offer fine views of the Wye and Elan valleys.

*Walk category* : Intermediate (3 hours).

*Length* : 11 km (7 miles).

WALK 4  PENRHIW - WEN

N

WYE
VALLEY

CERRIG-
GWALCH

MAEN SERTH ①

MAENGWYNGWEDDW ②

450m

400m

450m

Roman
Camp
Pool

500m

500m

Posts

Copse

½    1 Km.

½m.

½    ½m.

*Ascent* : 150 m (500 ft).

*Maps* : Landranger Sheet 143 or 136; Pathfinder 969 (SN 86/96) Rhayader and 1:25,000 First Series SN97 Llangurig.

*Starting and finishing point* : Leave Rhayader south-westward on the B4518, the road to the Elan valley. Just beyond Cwmdeuddwr, about 600 m from Rhayader's centre, a mountain road for Aberystwyth leaves rightwards. Take this. Beyond the forest the road climbs steadily. Park in one of the numerous lay-bys on this road, as close as possible to a point where the stream to the left runs into a small, dammed pond.

Further up the valley a rutted track heads off eastward. Take this and follow it up and across a plateau. Beyond at the top of a slight wide hill ahead the standing stone of Maen Serth is now visible. Leave the track when necessary to reach the stone (see (1) Maen Serth). Retrace the route to the plateau, then take an indistinct steep track that heads off right to contour along the cliffs of Cerrig-gwalch. At any suitable point, but best at about half-distance along the cliff, turn south-west (that is left, then half-left again) and head across the moor to a rutted track going north-west to south-east (that is left to right). Go right along this, passing a small, robust standing stone (see (2) Maengwyngweddw). Continue to the road.

Cross the road and take the gentle, left-curving ridge that rises on the other side. Follow this to its top and then turn south-eastward for the obvious top of Crugyn Ci across the boggy plateau ahead. Crugyn Ci has a trig point summit, which has to be searched for among the outcrops, and is a fine viewpoint (see (3) Crugyn Ci). The start point is just east of north from the peak, but the easiest way is offered by a trio of modern concrete posts that point towards a small copse. Follow that line until a vague track is reached that contours the hillside. Go left along it, and leave it at any convenient point where the steepish valley side can be descended. To the left as you descend, beyond the obvious sheepfold, are the remains of a Roman fort similar to that on Penycrocbren hill on Walk 3, and equally elusive to the amateur's eye. It is said that from the air, or when there is a light snow covering, it is plainly visible. Cross the stream easily, but with care, to regain the start.

(1) *Maen Serth*

Standing stones have held a fascination for man ever since their original erection, certainly by the Bronze Age and perhaps as early as the neolithic. Even today there is a power in such stones, particularly when, as here, they stand in isolated, romantic splendour. Maen Serth is the 'steep stone', a tall monolith that dominates the skyline for much of the early part of our walk. The slight ambiguity over the age of the monolith is not helped by a find from a cairn near it and, indeed, on our route, but too damaged to be of any interest to, or even to be recognised by, the layman. At Clap-y-arian a stone axe was found, but of a design favoured by the Beaker folk, Bronze Age builders of Stonehenge, who knew how to use metal, but had insufficient of it for their needs. Mention of Stonehenge is of interest here, as the axe was found to be of Preseli stone, perhaps from a Stonehenge bluestone quarry. The axe also suggests a cross-country trade route – what a fine walk that would be if it were rediscovered.

In the late twelfth century the country around Rhayader was disputed by Roger Mortimer, the local Norman Marcher lord, and the Welsh chieftains Rhys ap Gruffydd and the brothers Cadwallon and Einion Clud. The dispute spilled over into occasional violence but earned each man the respect of the others. Consequently at Christmas 1176 all four men gathered at Rhys's castle to feast and joust. Einion Clud defeated Roger Mortimer in the joust, the Norman lord showing his contempt for good sportsmanship by ambushing the Welshman as he returned home. Einion Clud was killed – as was his brother a little later, also by Mortimer – on this Elenydd ridge. Traditionally the killing was at Maen Serth, which has also been known locally as the Prince's Stone. Interestingly *serth* is also Welsh for obscene, a meaning which a murder site could easily assume.

After the death a cross was incised on the stone as a memorial, though it is now almost impossible to see the carving beneath the lichen cover. But there is another interpretation of the events, see Note (2) below.

(2) *Maengwyngweddw*

This shorter, harder, less conspicuous stone stands closer to the road and

Maen Serth

below a small ridge – a much more convenient place for an ambush than the site of Maen Serth. Another version of the Einion Clud murder story outlined in Note (1) above has Clud murdered here, the stone being named for his surviving wife, the White Stone of the Widow.

That leaves the problem of the incised cross on Maen Serth, but there is yet another tradition that a medieval judge was murdered there *en route* to, or from, the Rhayader assize, and that the cross commemorates his killing. A more prosaic explanation is that the carving was the 'Christianising' of a pagan monolith, an attempt by an awe–struck populace to reduce the power of the stone. Many examples of this are known, from the intricate carving of crosses on the tops of huge menhirs in Brittany to the church-led, ritual destruction of stones from the Avebury circle, a ritual which lasted until only a century or two ago.

(3) *Crugyn Ci*

As a viewpoint Crugyn Ci suffers from a plateau-like summit that hides from the walker a view of the Elan valley reservoirs. However, the deep gash of the valley itself is visible, as is the huge expanse of rolling moorland of Elenydd. Away from the moor the Wye valley offers a fine view eastward.

## Walk 5 (a) The Afon Ystwyth (b) Cwmystwyth

Further west along the mountain road to Aberystwyth that took us to the start of the walk to Maen Serth are two fine short walks that explore the varied country and heritage of the northern end of Elenydd. Both take the banks of the Afon Ystwyth, but they could hardly be more dissimilar.

*Walk category* : (a) Easy ($^1/_2$ hour); (b) Easy ($^1/_2$ hour).

*Length* : (a) $1^1/_2$ km (1 mile); (b) $2^1/_2$ km ($1^1/_2$ miles).

*Ascent* : (a) 20 m (60 ft); (b) Flat.

*Maps* : (a) and (b) Landranger Sheet 135 or 136; 1:25,000 First Series
         SN87 Afon Elan.

WALKS 5a. & b. YSTWYTH VALLEY-

AFON DILUW

(S5a)

N ←

NANT TROED-Y-RHIW

COPA HILL

NANT YR ONEN
5a ①

AFON YSTWYTH

½        ½ m

1 Km

CWMYSTWYTH
MINE
5a ②

(S5b)

## (a) The Afon Ystwyth

Westward from Maen Serth the mountain road reaches the head of the
Craig Goch reservoir where the Elan valley road turns left (south) over
Pont ar Elan. Continuing along the mountain road the visitor follows the
old turnpike, passing, at 871 741 the ruins of Hillgate, an old toll-gate
house. Hillgate was destroyed during the local Rebecca Riots of 1843-4
when the locals, dressed as women with blackened faces, took their
name from the Old Testament character and the Testament's advice that
they should rise up and possess the gates of their oppressors. The rioters
were protesting about the iniquities of the turnpike system which forced
the locals to pay tolls for the use of roads that were never maintained.

*Starting and finishing point :* West again from the ruins of Hillgate there
is a fine bog, Gors Lwyd, to the left. Beyond, the road swings leftward
and reaches, at 849 757, a small pull-in to the right.

From the pull-in go down over steepish, slightly boggy ground to the
stream, the fledgling Afon Ystwyth, and follow it to its confluence with
the Afon Diluw. Follow the river downstream for any distance from a
few hundred metres to 1 km ($\frac{1}{2}$ mile). The river is very beautiful, with
occasional water-hollowed rocks and fine plant life. The far riverside has
a path that leads back up the Afon Diluw, but the crossing of the Afon
Ystwyth is not easy unless the water level is very low.

## (b) Cwmystwyth

Westward from the start of Walk 5(a) are the ruins of the Cwmystwyth
mine. This is an eerie site, and also a very dangerous one for the unwary
or for unrestrained children. It is also a fascinating site, and perfectly
safe if sensible precautions are observed.

*Starting and finishing point :* At any of a number of sites near (803 745),
at the western end of the mining site.

From the start go down to the river and, turning left (eastward), follow it

The Afon Ystwyth

upstream to the far end of the mine site. This is recognisable from the steep gash through the rocks above the mine site that brings the Nant yr Onen stream (see (1) Nant yr Onen) down to the Afon Ystwyth. The Nant forces the walker on to the road which gives access to the mine site, its huge tips, shafts, pools and rubbish. With caution the walker can visit the sites (see (2) Cwmystwyth Mine), experiencing at first hand the desolation. But please beware – of all buildings, which are very unstable, of old shafts, some of which are partially filled and so look innocuous, and of the occasional unsatisfactory heap of old rubbish that has the potential to badly cut the slipping leg.

(1) *Nant yr Onen*
The Cwmystwyth Mine produced not only lead but copper, the copper ore being chiefly found on Copper Hill drained on its western side by the Nant yr Onen. Interestingly the hill's name is now most frequently rendered as Copa Hill, *copa* being Welsh for a crest. This is barely acceptable geographically and it seems more likely to be a 'Welshised' version of the English name. The hill's copper ore was exposed by hushing, a process in which artificial reservoirs were created on the hillside, the water in them being released quickly to scour away the topsoil of the hill and so reveal the ore. The hushing scars that radiate out from the Nant yr Onen are believed to be the finest remains of the technique in Britain.

(2) *Cwmystwyth Mine*
In 1872 the Cwmystwyth Mine was noted as being 'both the richest and the oldest wrought mine in the county (of Cardiganshire)' and as having produced, by that time, more than two million pounds' worth of lead ore. That money came from the extraction and crushing of perhaps 100,000 tons of rock. In its early days the mine shafts for lead ore were dug horizontally into the hillside, vertical shafts only being introduced when a 30-ft waterwheel was erected to power pumps to extract water, seepage always being a local problem. By the last years of the nineteenth century the mine was finding it hard to compete, and it finally closed in 1921. Those interested in learning more of the local mining industry should go

west from the site, then northward on the B4574 to Devil's Bridge and on to Ponterwyd on the A44. Go left there to reach the Llywernog Mining Museum.

   More details of the mine are available in Part 1 of David Bick's fine series *The Old Metal Mines of Mid-Wales*.

## Walk 6 The Teifi Pools

This route takes a narrow, no-through road that penetrates deeply into Elenydd from the west, using a series of small pools to act as a guide through some lovely, but lonely countryside, reminiscent of deepest Elenydd, but more 'user-friendly'. That said, the going is a little uncompromising, turning an easy walk into one requiring a little more effort.

*Walk category* : Easy/Intermediate (2 hours).

*Length* : 7 km (4$\frac{1}{2}$ miles).

*Ascent* : 50 m (160 ft).

*Maps* :  Landranger Sheets 135 or 147; Pathfinder 968 (SN66/76)
          Bronnant and Pontrhydfendigaid.

*Starting and finishing point* : Take the road that leaves the B4343 eastward at the inn in Ffair Rhos, a little north of Pontrhydfendigaid. Follow the narrow, occasionally blind-bended, road for about 2$\frac{1}{2}$ miles. After a steep rise there is a zig-zag across a bridge. Park at a pull-in on the right, beyond the bridge, at 779 682.

Follow the road – but do not walk on it, take the verge to one side or the other – among some magnificent rock scenery to a lane right that leads to Llyn Egnant, the last of the pools. This lane is the third to the right, and is recognisable as being just before the road peters out into an undrivable – except by four-wheel drive – moorland track. Go down the reservoir lane, passing the whole length of Llyn Egnant. Go ahead on a

# WALK 6 THE TEIFI POOLS

N

450m

S

LLYN
TEIFI (1)

LLYN
HIR

PEN Y
BRYN

S

LLYN
EGNANT

400m

450m

LLYN y
GORLAN

LLYN BACH

450m

G

½     1 Km

½ m

still distinct track, passing a waymarker, to a gate. Go through, and follow the fence rightward. The fence turns sharp right – go with it and follow it as it curves leftward. At a second obvious right turn leave the fence, which goes on to meet Llyn y Gorlan, to head for an obvious pass between small hillocks. Beyond is another similar pass. Go through this, then up and right over a ridge to reach Llyn Teifi (see (1) Teifi Pools). Go around Llyn Teifi's southern end, following a concrete wall, which can be walked, towards the dam turret. Just before it, go left to follow and cross a stream to reach a stile over a fence.

Go over the stile, turning half-left beyond to reach the final dam wall, a construction more remarkable for its brutal pragmatism than its charm. Go round the last pool on its western side, avoiding its northern end which is very boggy. Instead make for a long, shallow grassy ridge to the left that leads back to the pull-in.

## (1) *Teifi Pools*

The area of land around the pools is reckoned to be the finest stretch of high, wild grassland left in the high mid-Wales plateau that has not disappeared under forestry. The land would originally have been forested, clearing and the introduction of sheep having eliminated that cover, but the present wildness is to be preferred to the regimented rows of conifer. Away from the pools navigation can be a problem, with the hills all looking a little the same, the rock outcrops likewise, and the myriad small valleys and passes hindering rather than helping the walker. This geography does however produce ideal country for wheatears and buzzards, ravens and even the elusive kite. In addition the bogs that surround and separate the pools prevent over-grazing and allow some really fine plants to maintain a hold. The walker will delight in finding his own favourite, but do look for the bog rosemary with its tiny, pink bell-like flowers.

# Southern Elenydd

South of the Teifi Pools the highland of Elenydd is very heavily wooded, especially in the centre, where the Tywi Forest and its northern continuation stretch virtually continuously from a point about 4 km ($2^1/_2$ miles) south of the pools all the way to the Llyn Brianne reservoir, and after a very short break on south to Llanwrtyd Wells. To the east of this huge forest area there is a fine moorland area around Drygarn Fawr, at 645 m (2116 ft), the highest peak of Elenydd. Access to this area is not difficult, as the roads to the north – the Claerwen reservoir road – and south – the mountain road from Beulah to Tregaron – are largely unfenced. The walking is rough, however, and there are a limited number of objectives and landmarks: it is land to walk across rather than around.

To the west of the area there is another huge forestry plantation, the Cwm Berwyn Forest, north-west of which is Cors goch, Tregaron Bog. This peat bog, formed where a post-glacial lake once lay, is a naturalist's dream for its bog plant-life, butterflies, dragonflies, damselflies and migrating birds – over 160 species have been recorded. A path crosses an edge of the bog, but this gives the only access and barely constitutes a Best Walk.

Between the forests of Cwm Berwyn and Tywi there is a fine, if narrow, piece of moorland. Here are Ty'n-y-cornel, one of Wales' most remote Youth Hostels, and Soar y Mynydd, one of its most remote chapels. Excellent long walks link these sites and others, crossing the moors and visiting the upper valley of the Doethie and Pysgotwr rivers, but again the general lie of the land and positions of access roads make short, circular walks difficult. South again are the valleys of the Gwenffrwd, Cothi and Tywi rivers forming an almost continuous circle around the high land of Mynydd Mallaen. These valleys offer some of the most beautiful wooded scenery in Wales – the drive from Pumsaint to Llandovery via Rhandirmwyn is one of the very best in Wales. The Cothi valley is reckoned by many to be the finest in Wales, though competition for that title is fierce and the Wye valley has sufficient admirers to ensure a victory in most polls. Nonetheless it is a fine valley, spoilt for the walker by access difficulties, few metres of its banks having footpaths. Sadly the same is true for most of the Gwenffrwd and Tywi valleys too, and we restrict ourselves here to two short walks that explore different aspects of the scenery of southern Elenydd.

## Walk 7 The Cothi Valley

The Cothi valley is a delight, a beautiful wooded valley running down from below the crags of Craig Branddu. Access to the river banks is severely restricted, but at a point near the village of Pumsaint the walker can get quite close, if only for a short distance. To produce a circular walk it is necessary to use roads to return to the start point, but these are quiet country lanes with views of the valley as good as any to be had, and offer the distinct advantage of a visit to the Roman gold mines of Dolaucothi.

*Walk Category* : Easy ($1^3/_4$ hours).

*Length* : 6 km ($3^3/_4$ miles).

*Ascent* :  60 m (200 ft).

*Maps* :  Landranger Sheet 146; Pathfinder Sheet 1013 (SN 64/74) Cilycwm and Pumsaint.

*Starting and finishing point* : The village of Pumsaint on the A482 from Llanwrda to Lampeter. There is also a National Trust car park at the Dolaucothi Gold Mine, at 663  403, just off the main road, a little south of Pumsaint. This car-park is for visitors to the mine and so must be used with discretion. If it is largely empty, and you are intending to visit the mine after the walk, there would seem to be little harm.

From the village go south towards the bridge over the Cothi, but before reaching it go left on a lane signed for Dolaucothi Farm (bed, breakfast and evening meal). Anyone looking for somewhere for an overnight stay

*Sheep shearing in the Cothi valley*

need look no further. Follow the lane until another signed lane for the farm leads off right. The actual right of way does not follow this lane, but leaves the main lane about 150 m further on. This 'real' path is not easy to locate, however, and custom and practice take the walker down the farm access lane. Where the lane splits take the left fork. At its end go right, through the farmyard. Go down to a stile over a fence, noting the direction of the yellow arrow. Several stiles have these arrows and as the path is occasionally indistinct they are a useful guide.

Bear left after the first stile, following the left-hand hedge to another stile. Over this go left and up a steepish bank to where a marker post points to another stile. Beyond yet another stile there are two distinct, if not well-worn, paths ahead. The upper one goes along an avenue of trees, while the lower one goes down towards the river before rising again. Both paths meet at a stile, beyond which the path, after descending towards the river, rises to go above a crumbling embankment. Care is needed here, particularly if the weather has been wet. Beyond this section a piece of rough ground must be crossed to a footbridge over the Cothi. Here, at last, the full beauty of the valley is revealed. Over the bridge bear right with the fence, leaving it to go left of an old shed to reach a gate into Llandre Farm. Go across the yard and out of another gate. Go right and follow the road to Carreg Pumsaint, to the left (see (1) Carreg Pumsaint) and the entrance to the mine (see (2) Dolaucothi Gold Mine). Continue to a triangle road junction. The first road here is signed 'No Entry', but walkers are exempt. Take the road and follow it to the main A482. Go right for the last few metres into Pumsaint, pausing for one last look from the Cothi bridge.

### (1) *Carreg Pumsaint*

Pumsaint is almost Welsh for five saints. I say almost because although *pum* is the correct adjectival rendering of *pump*, for five, the Welsh for saint is *sant*, without the 'i'. It is clear however that the name is derived from an ancient legend that five Celtic saints set up a hermitage here in the Cothi valley. Of that original site nothing now remains and more extraordinarily there is no church within the village. This stone, Carreg Pumsaint, is said to have been a shelter for the saints, the hollows having been formed by their heads and shoulders. Sadly for this fine story there

# WALK 7 — THE COTHI VALLEY

FOOTBRIDGE

LLANDRE FARM

150m

BRUNANT

N

S

S

S

150m

S

DOLAUCOTHI FARM

S

PUMSAINT

S

½    1 Km

½ m

CARREG PUMSAINT ①

150m

DOLAUCOTHI GOLD MINE ②

are only four sets of impressions. Originally the marks were believed to be cup marks, a not-infrequent carving on menhirs, and the stone was assumed to be ancient. Today it is more widely believed that the stone has stood on the site for less than 200 years and that the impressions are from its use as an anvil in an ore-crushing machine, perhaps as lately as the sixteenth century.

The wooded mound beside the site is thought by some to be a Norman motte, but others contend that it is more likely to be a pile of mining waste! Slag heap not castle, anvil not miracle stone. So much for romance.

### (2) Dolaucothi Gold Mine

Because of their experience with gold mining on mainland Europe – particularly in northern Spain where their techniques were described in detail by Pliny the Elder, techniques which match those employed at Dolaucothi – the Romans would have quickly realised the potential of the site here. The Roman extraction technique involved hushing (see Note (1) of Walk 5(b)) to remove the topsoil and surface rock, and this required huge quantities of water. This was taken from the Cothi several miles upstream and brought here by a brilliantly engineered aqueduct whose line can still be traced, in places, on the east side of the Cothi valley. Just south of Llandre Farm on our walk, and again on the east side of the valley, there was a holding tank that would hold one million litres (200,000 gallons) of water. Release of all or some of this scoured away the rock, the scoured flow being directed into channels that were partially dammed with gorse. The heavy gold fragments were filtered out by the gorse which was then burnt to release the metal. And in case all of this sounds very fanciful, the same technique was being employed to extract gold from near-surface veins only two centuries ago.

When the gold veins went underground the Romans would have followed them by trenching. To break up the rock more quickly than manual techniques could manage they lit fires to heat the rock, then cooled it with water to crack it. Close to the surface this technique is reasonable, but when carried out below ground it is a very hazardous procedure and, probably, slave labour would have been used. Water

Carreg Pumsaint

seepage would have been a problem once the mining was below the surface, and the Romans built waterwheels to pump the water out. It was the discovery of the remains of one of these wheels in the 1930s that confirmed Roman involvement at the site, though there had been local discoveries of superb gold jewellery.

From Roman times onwards there were sporadic attempts to find an elusive lode at Dolaucothi, the techniques employed being, as noted above, so similar that it is difficult to say with certainty which mining efforts are Roman and which are from the seventeenth century. More recently there were half-a-dozen attempts to mine from the mid-nineteenth century onwards. The last, and one of the most determined, was in the 1930s. Ironically this attempt failed, in 1938, shortly after the production of the first 100-ounce gold bar.

Today the Dolaucothi site is in the care of the National Trust. Visitors are kitted out with clothing, helmets and lamps and taken on a tour of the underground mine workings, a most interesting experience. For those not happy with enclosed spaces there is also a surface route, visiting the most important parts of the site. Refreshments are available.

## Walk 8 Dinas

North of Pumsaint the visitor can follow the Cothi valley past Cwrt-y-Cadno and under the crags of Craig Branddu to where the road leaves it as the river makes a right-angled turn from north-east to north-west. A footpath from near the telephone box here follows the river for a short way, passing Pwll Uffern-Cothi, Hell's Pool on the Cothi, thought by many researchers to be the source of water for the Roman aqueduct that fed Dolaucothi (see Walk 7). Beyond the point where the Cothi heads off there is a short rise and on the fall beyond, over Bwlch-y-rhiw, we have crossed the watershed and the streams drain east to the Tywi. The first stream here is the Nant Melyn, which soon joins the Gwenffrwd. This river flows through land that was the scene of the joyously successful programme of the Royal Society for the Protection of Birds (RSPB) to save the red kite. A second RSPB site, and the site of our

walk, is reached by crossing the Rhandirmwyn bridge just after the Gwenffrwd has joined the Afon Doethie.

*Walk Category* : Easy (1 hour).

*Length* : $3^1/_2$ km (2 miles).

*Ascent* :  60 m (200 ft).

*Maps* :  Landranger Sheets 146 or 147; Pathfinder Sheet 1013 (SN 64/ 74) Cilycwm and Pumsaint.

*Starting and finishing point* : The RSPB car-park at 786 472 reached either by the route from Pumsaint as described above or from Llandovery. From Llandovery take the minor road northward for Rhandirmwyn continuing through that small village towards Llyn Brianne. The car-park is to the left, signed for the RSPB, after the church of St Paulinus has been passed.

At the bottom left-hand corner of the car-park a kissing gate leads to a raised wooden walkway that wends its way for around 400 m up on to the wooded hillside of Dinas. The walkway gives access to a boggy area that would otherwise be completely inaccessible. The visitor therefore has a very close view of some excellent bog plants. In exchange, the walkway can be a bit slippery if it is wet, especially on the uphill sections, despite the added metal mesh designed to provide a better grip. It also runs close to an overhanging bush at one point and has passing places because of its single-line-traffic nature. A real adventure. As the walkway ends paths go left and right. One is the outward route, one the return. It is best, I feel, to go right first, to walk with the river, but as the river section of the journey is undoubtedly the best many may prefer to go left, so as to leave it until last.

   Rightward the river, the Afon Tywi, is soon reached, the route climbing along the steep hillside above it. The river here is beautiful beyond superlatives, the craggy outcrops of Pen Rhiwbie adding a splendid backdrop to the view. The path along the hillside of Dinas (see (1) Dinas) at this point is rugged. There are occasional side-paths but please keep to the way-marked – look for yellow direction arrows on wooden posts – route. There are stepped sections and occasional forays over slimy, angular rocks that are very slippery in the wet. Be cautious too if approaching the river where the boulders are equally slippery if wet and the water cold and swift-moving, not nice as a landing spot.

At length the Afon Tywi is joined by the Afon Doethie and after following the combined rivers at greater distance the path swings left around the south side of Dinas entering a more genteel wooded section. Eventually the walkway is reached again, and followed back to the car-park and RSPB Information Centre (see (2) RSPB reserve). To complete a good half-day the visitor can now visit a couple of local sites (see (3) Other places of interest).

## (1) *Dinas*

*Dinas* means castle, although in Welsh it is frequently applied to natural rather than man-made fortresses. Here too the conical hill is a natural fortress, but with no direct evidence of its ever having been used as a defensive mound. Towards the summit on the northern side is a cave associated with Twm Siôn Catti, a Welsh Robin Hood. Twm was born in the early years of sixteenth century to Catherine Jones of Tregaron. Catherine named him Thomas John, Twm Siôn in Welsh, and as he was illegitimate, Catti was added to his name: he was Cathy's Tom John. In reality Twm was probably a Protestant, a rebel against the Catholic laws of Queen Mary, and it is known that he fled to Geneva around 1550. He returned to Wales and was granted a Royal Pardon in 1559, marrying the widow of the Sheriff of Carmarthen and living to a respectable old age. Later, in the eighteenth century, the romantic ideal of Twm the Outlaw grew up, with the man portrayed as a Robin Hood figure, though with considerably more humour and less tragedy than the English outlaw. The cave may never have been a base for Twm, but the Dinas site certainly has the correct romantic image.

## (2) *RSPB reserve*

In London in the Middle Ages the rubbish-strewn streets were scavenged by a fork-tailed bird of prey, the red kite. Persecution and, later, hygiene forced the kite back to its country home, where it was further persecuted by gamekeepers and farmers. The bird is a nervous nester and disturbances at nest sites also took their toll. By the early years of this century it was thought that the kite was extinct in Britain, but a few pairs, perhaps as few as five or six, clung tenaciously to what remained of their range, the moorlands around the wooded nesting valleys of the Gwenffrwd and the Doethie streams. The birds' 'discovery' not so many years ago, when attitudes to wildlife among the general public were changing, caused a stir and the struggle to protect them and to increase their number became a *cause célèbre*.

The walkway in the Dinas Reserve

The RSPB's part in the recovery, which involved the buying of Dinas in 1968, has been significant. Ironically the bird no longer nests in the two original valleys, but its range and numbers have increased. It is now seen as far north as the Dyfi and often drifts much further afield. Visitors to Dinas always have a chance of seeing the bird. From a distance it is distinguished from the more common buzzard by its deeply forked tail; closer, by its colour – gorgeous chestnut. Usually the bird is seen working the thermals above scarp slopes looking for its prey of small animals and birds. It also takes snakes, a habit that led one nineteenth century egg collector to warn of half-dead adders near its nest.

Over forty species of bird breed regularly in the sessile oakwoods and surrounding countryside of Dinas. Chief among these are the pied flycatcher and redstart, with dippers and yellow wagtails near the Tywi. The RSPB has numbered marker posts on the walk with an explanatory leaflet of what can be seen. I shall not repeat the information: the visitor should obtain the leaflet from the Information Centre, where we can also take out a year's membership of the society. Dinas is a magnificent site: it and the society need your support.

(3) *Other places of interest*

St Paulinus church, near the car-park entrance, was built originally in the early twelfth century, but has been much restored, chiefly by the Cowder family. It is a simple, dignified building more pleasing for its exterior and its position than for its interior.

About 2 km (1 mile) north of the reserve is Llyn Brianne, a recent reservoir completed in 1972 and holding about 50,000 million litres (13,000 million gallons) of water. From the viewing point and picnic area just below the top of the dam the 'flip-bucket' water discharge looks very attractive. In addition to water flowing down the dam's spillway, some water is taken by pipe to the dam's base and turned up in the air to form a huge cone, not unlike a fountain for ping-pong balls at a fairground. In the right conditions a huge rainbow sits across the fountain and the visitor is wetted by the escaping spray. One advantage of the arrangement is that it oxygenates the water of the Tywi which helps the water life considerably.

The Afon Tywi

# The Radnor Forest

To the east of the Elan valley the mid-Wales plateau is dissected into smaller blocks by river valleys that hold the main access roads from South to North Wales. Around Llanbadarn Fynydd the block is slightly lower and more fertile, the land more cultivated and access slightly more difficult. This block is crossed by Owain Glyndwr's Way which visits Abbey Cwmhir, a magnificent – and historically important – monastic site, spoiled by poor preservation and indifferent planning decisions.

Southward is a second, smaller block, the Radnor Forest. Old Radnor, well set on a rocky ridge, has an ancient history, though when the Normans came they set their castle at New Radnor, to the west. This new site was the start of *The Journey through Wales* of Gerald of Wales and Archbishop Baldwin and, typically of the man, Gerald recounts a local anecdote about the castellan, or captain, of the castle in the time of Henry I. The captain spent a night in a local church, together with his dogs, and for this irreverence his dogs were driven mad and he was struck blind. After several years of misery he journeyed to Jerusalem hoping not for a cure, but for a chance of spiritual redemption. He reached the city during an upsurge in fighting between Christians and Muslims, requested that he be strapped on to his horse and taken to the battlefield. He rode at the infidel army and was promptly killed. Gerald records, with satisfaction, that the captain's life thus ended with honour.

A later king, Charles I, stayed locally on the night of 6 August 1645 and was poorly fed at an inn called The Bush. Even the miserly ration of cheese he was offered was taken from him before he had eaten properly. The king, not amused, noted that the place should really be called Beggar's Bush, and so it still is, the name having transferred to a small hamlet a few miles north-east of New Radnor.

The Radnor Forest was a forest in the ancient name, a hunting ground, though lately the extensive forestry plantations on the north and south sides have given the old name a new meaning. It is a small, square area, no more than 6 km (4 miles) on the side, with lovely little partially-penetrating valleys. The highest points, Black Mixen and Great Rhos,

are not on public rights of way – though Forestry Commission paths are gradually opening the area - and much of the map is covered with 'DANGER AREA' to warn visitors off the Radnor range. We take the hint, visiting one delightful valley, set in the heart of a forest area noted for its balance of tree species, to see a fine waterfall, Water-Break-Its-Neck.

## Walk 9 Water-Break-Its-Neck

*Walk category* : Easy (2 hours).

*Length* : 6 km (4 miles).

*Ascent* : 140 m (450 ft).

*Maps* : Landranger Sheet 148; Pathfinder Sheets 992 (SO 05/15) Builth Wells and 970(SO 06/16) Llandrindod Wells.

*Starting and finishing point* : At 198 598 on the A44 Llandrindod Wells to Kington road. About 2 km (1$^1/_2$ miles) south-west of New Radnor is a lay-by with an AA telephone box. Start here.

Walk south along the main road for about 500 m, passing a lane to Vron Farm, to a stony lane right. Take this and follow it to a Y-junction. Here take the right track, signed for the waterfall, a forestry road that leads to a large vehicle-turning area where the stream – Black Brook – from the waterfall goes under the track. Technically it is possible to drive to this point, and many people do, but the drive is across private forestry land and there are occasional signs, much vandalised, that record the privacy. Those who do drive risk a confrontation. From the turning area the waterfall (see Note (1) Water-Break-Its-Neck) can be reached by following the path upstream – crossing it by means of a nice log bridge – for only about 100 m. Our walk continues by taking the left track at another Y-junction just beyond the stream. The track rises steeply and steadily to a point where a path goes sharply left. Take this to a farm building. Go left around the farm on an indistinct path that becomes more distinct as it drops steeply towards Black Brook.

Beyond a people-retaining wire fence, a steep path drops off the main path to reach a stone mushroom viewpoint above the waterfall. The main path crosses the Brook by way of an elegant footbridge, rising muddily, then falling through fine woodland to reach the outward track. Go right to reverse the outward journey.

## (1) *Water-Break-Its-Neck*

The elegantly named fall drops about 50 m (80 ft) over a sill of hard rock. In dry weather the stream, which has come only a short distance from its source, is a mere trickle and the waterfall is much less imposing than its name. After heavy rain however the volume is considerable and the falls are a fine sight. The valley below the falls is tight; the lack of sun and damp conditions have developed a rich variety of mosses and plants, some growing on exposed patches of rock. Elsewhere on the walk there are magnificent trees – note especially the Scots Pine where the lane to the farm is taken, the larches and the fine examples of Californian Redwood.

# The Pembrokeshire Coast National Park

To the west of Wales two arms of land enclose, pincer-like, a huge area of the Irish or Celtic Sea. The enclosed sea forms Cardigan Bay, the arms being the Lleyn Peninsula in the north and the wider, blunter snout of old Pembrokeshire to the south. The blunt snout of Pembrokeshire is itself divided, the headlands near St David's and further south near Marloes enclosing St Bride's Bay, a miniature of the larger Cardigan Bay. South again the long inlet of Milford Haven, one of the world's finest natural harbours, separates the southern tip of the old county, an area from Pembroke down to Tenby, from the main county bulk, creating what is virtually an island of land.

The rocks of Pembrokeshire are a geology lesson in themselves, there being representative masses of all the major geological eras from Pre-Cambrian to Recent, with a predominance of older rocks to the north and younger rocks to the south. While the underlying geology affects the scenery it is at the coast that the layman gets his most obvious glimpse of the rocks. Southern Pembrokeshire has cliffs of Carboniferous limestone, an acid-dissolvable rock that has been etched by the sea into steep, jagged cliffs, constant weathering also producing a fine series of arches and towers. Further north the rocks are softer slates, easily weathered into smooth bays separated by cliffs of harder, unyielding rocks, some igneous in nature. The magnificent seascapes offered by these rock types, together with the pastoral beauty of inland Pembrokeshire and the existence of offshore islands that were important bird reserves led the National Parks Commission to designate the county's coast a National Park in 1952. The decision was, to date, unique, all of the other National Parks of England and Wales being inland, mountain areas. The decision was correct however, and far-sighted, the coastline here being perhaps the finest in the two countries, rivalled only by that in Cornwall. The whole of the coast is included in the Park, apart from a small section around the busy ferry harbour of Fishguard. The decision to include all, rather than specific parts, means that the full range of varied coastal scenery is included, as too are the islands of Skomer, Skokholm and Ramsey, and that the spiritual home of Wales, the cathedral village-city of St David's, lies within the Park's protective boundaries.

Equally far-sighted was the decision to deviate inland at one point in the north of the old county in order to include in the National Park the Preseli Hills. These hills, though neither spectacularly beautiful, nor either high or extensive, are one of the most interesting prehistoric sites in Britain, the more so since the extraordinary discovery that the sandstone of Stonehenge was quarried from the range's eastern end.

Almost two decades after the designation of the National Park – the Coast Park was the fifth to be so designated and is still Britain's smallest, at 580 square km (225 square miles) – the Countryside Commission gave final approval to a long-distance footpath around the coast from Amroth on the old county border with Carmarthenshire to St Dogmael's on the old border with Cardiganshire. This is a superb walk, and while it does not visit all of the interesting places in this remote and mysterious area, it does give an excellent view of a peninsula that the ancient Welsh knew as *gwlad hud a lledrith*, the land of magic and enchantment.

## Walk 10 St David's

The southernmost pincer that encloses Cardigan Bay comprises a broad headland, itself composed of a number of headlands. St David's Head is the most northerly of these small promontories and southward from it is the magnificent sandy sweep of Whitesands Bay. Our route, a part of the official Pembrokeshire Coastal Path, takes the southern headland, which has few sandy bays – and access to those that there are is difficult – but offers superb rock scenery, a fine view of Ramsey Island, the advantage of walking around enough degrees of the compass to ensure that at least part of it is wind-free, and a chance to visit St David's itself, the spiritual heart of Christian Wales.

*Walk category* : Intermediate ($3^1/_2$ hours).

*Length* : 15 km (9 miles).

*Ascent* :  90 m (300 ft).

*Maps* : Landranger Sheet 157; Pathfinder Sheet 1005 (SM62/72)
            St David's (Tyddewi) and Ramsey Island.

*Starting and finishing point* : There are several. There is a car-park at
724 251 near St Justinian's, and another at 751 244 near St Non's. Better
than either, and much bigger than either, is that at 750 254 used by
visitors to St David's Cathedral. It is a pay park, but is nicely situated
beside a stream and allows a leisurely visit to St David's either before or
after the walk.

The car-park is reached over a narrow bridge at the bottom of a steep,
signed road from the village-city of St David's. Continue along the road
to the park, a quiet country lane with fine hedgerows. To the left, after
about 1 km ($^1/_2$ mile), the small hillock of Clegyr-Boia is topped by the
remains of a hill fort (see (3) Porthlysgi). At the road end there is a car-
park, St Justinian's and the first view of Ramsey Island (see (1) St
Justinian and Ramsey Island). Steps left, beside a waymarker, give
access to the coastal path which is followed easily all the way around the
headland. In springtime this section of the coast is pure yellow with
gorse which is packed tight against the path. There is so much that on
still, warm days it can be smelt, a sweet, warm smell, vaguely reminding
the walker of an exotic, cooked dessert in a five-star restaurant. Among
the gorse there are yellow-hammers and stonechats.

   Castell Heinif fort is passed (see (2) Castell Heinif), beyond which the
walker is usually alone with the air and the view. After the headland of
Penmaenmelyn, the most westerly point on mainland Wales, has been
rounded there is a proliferation of paths near the bay of Ogof Cadno. At
this point, and at occasional others along the way, all paths eventually
rejoin, though to be absolutely safe take the one that is closest to the cliff
edge. Beyond Ogof Cadno – *ogof* here being used in its sense of cavern,
or steep-sided, rocky hollow, rather than cave, the usual meaning – is
another rock-cut bay, the delightfully named Ogof Mrs Morgan. It is
believed, but without true justification, that Mrs Morgan was associated
in some way with the copper mines a little inland from here. Also inland
is a small pond, the first of several, used for the irrigation of
Pembrokeshire early potatoes.

Beyond the pool at 724 236 the path uses concrete slabs to cross boggy ground to reach a signpost. Ahead is a fine section of cliff, rounding Maes Llwydwyn to reach the sheltered bay of Porthlysgi (see (3) Porthlysgi). Here is a beach that is far enough from roads to be almost always empty. Offshore is Bishop's Rock, one of many so named. Beyond, the cliff is more vegetated to Porth Clais (see (4) Porth Clais), an infuriatingly long inlet. On this section the author was once startled by a young adder that crossed the path where he was least expecting one – perhaps you will be as lucky.

Porth Clais offers a superb seaweedy smell as it is entered, but an altogether more dubious smell as it is left. Beyond the latter smell is excellent cliff all the way to St Non's. As the retreat and the chapel ruins come into view, watch for a step-through in the fence to the left that gives access to a grassy path that passes the chapel (see (5) St Non's) to reach the well. From the well a track leads to a car-park. Go left on the road to reach St David's.

Go right when the city is reached, then left at the 'village green' and left again at the surfing gallery to reach the head of a flight of steps leading down to the cathedral (see (6) St David's). Beyond the cathedral is the Bishop's Palace, a lane between the two offering a return to the start.

(1) *St Justinian and Ramsey Island*
The harbour here is, in Welsh, Porthstinian, though locally it is frequently called St Justinian. The saint in question was a Breton hermit who, traditionally, arrived in Pembrokeshire towards the end of St David's life and acted as his confessor. He became abbot of St David's monastery but was appalled at the lack of commitment of the monks there and left to become a hermit on Ramsey Island. Some of the monks followed him, but became weary of his iron discipline and in a show of far from Christian compassion they cut off the saint's head. St Justinian's body picked up the head and walked with it across Ramsey Sound to this delightful harbour where the awe-struck locals buried both body and head and raised a chapel. The chapel became a place of pilgrimage, but fell into disuse and disrepair. St Justinian's remains were then taken to St David's Cathedral. During the Civil War Cromwell's

RAMSEY
ISLAND

RAMSEY

SOUND

ST JUSTINIAN ①

S

G
KG
CASTELL HEINIF ②

· · ·
THE
BITCHES

KG

×⊢ KG

POOLS

KG   S

PORTHLYSGI
BAY
③

KG   KG

KG   KG

OGOF CADNO

OGOF
MRS MORGAN

CARR
(Bı

BISHOP'S PALACE

CATHEDRAL

ST DAVID'S ⑥

Ⓢ

CLEGYR

KG

CHAPEL

ST NON'S ⑤

WELL

PORTH CLAIS ④

S

S

S

N

½        1 Km

½ m

men stole the bells from the chapel, but their ship foundered in Ramsey Sound, during a storm. Today in stormy weather it is said that the bells can still be heard. The chapel is on private land

Ramsey Island is probably named for a Viking settler, Hrafn. In Welsh the island was Ynys Dyfanog, Dyfanog being an early Celtic saint, but is now Ynys Dewi – St David's Isle – being by tradition the place where St David met St Patrick. It has a long Christian tradition, going back several centuries before St Justinian, perhaps as far back as the second century. In the sound between the island and the mainland there is a vicious tidal race, with currents of up to 8 knots. The sound is, not surprisingly, very dangerous, the dangers being added to by the series of sharp rocks that lie off the island's nearest point. These, The Bitches and The Whelps, are said to be the last remnants of the land bridge to the mainland. When St Justinian retreated to Ramsey he took an axe and broke up the land bridge behind him, but the axe became blunt and the last few strokes left slivers of rock behind. In fact Ramsey Sound is an ancient valley, ice-scoured in the last Ice Age and filled as the ice retreated. Today the island is a nature reserve administered by the Royal Society for the Protection of Birds and is home to more than thirty nesting species. Climbing on the sheer cliffs is *not* permitted, but boat trips visit the island in summer, leaving from St Justinian where the beautifully sited lifeboat station was built in 1911 – for just £3000.

## (2) *Castell Heinif*

The hessian-strung remains here are of an Iron Age fort. Typically these forts were built on hills and protected by an array of ramparts and ditches, but a promontory such as this had the natural advantage of being protected by sheer cliffs and the sea on two sides. A ditch and rampart section across the landward side thus gave total security for minimum labour. Near the fort is a superb natural rock arch.,

## (3) *Porthlysgi*

This bay or harbour is named for Lysgi, an Irish pirate who is said to have landed here and killed the local Celtic chief, Boia. Boia gave his name to Clegyr-Boia which our walk passed *en route* to St Justinian. Boia was head of a family who practised the ancient religion, perhaps

St Justinian's lifeboat station

druidism, and was in constant dispute with St David when he was establishing his first monastery. A story tells of Boia's wife, stepmother to his daughter, taking the daughter, Dunawd, off to gather nuts, and cutting her throat as she rested. Where the blood touched the earth a spring, Ffynnon Dunawd, rose. This helped convert Boia to Christianity – though in truth the story has gross pagan overtones. Sadly, Boia's conversion did not save him from Lysgi.

(4) *Porth Clais*

Porth Clais was the ancient harbour for St David's and must have seen a great deal of missionary and pilgrimage traffic in pre-Norman times. The Normans built a harbour here, landing the stone for the cathedral and the lead for the roof, the present breakwater being constructed on their foundations. Later the harbour was used for the import of coal for use in the local gasworks. The works has now been demolished, the remains at the quayside being of earlier kilns used to supply local farmers with lime. The river that flows into the harbour is the Alun that also flows beside the car-park where our walk started. Near the bridge over the river is the little that remains of Ffynnon Dewi – David's Well. Here the saint was baptised, a spring starting miraculously for the event. At the baptism a blind man held David, and his sight was restored during the baby's immersion. Those familiar with the *Mabinogion* that wonderful collection of Celtic myth and legend through which drifts a tantalisingly elusive whiff of ancient folklore and which includes many tales about Arthur, will remember that Twrch Trywyth, the Irish boar which fought Arthur and his Knights, landed at Porth Clais after swimming from Ireland.

(5) *St Non's*

St Non was the mother of St David, and tradition has it that the chapel ruins in the field are the site of the patron saint's birth. Non was the wife of Sant, a grandson of Cunedda and a local prince. Their home was here, close to the headland of Trwyn Cynddeiriog, Fury Point, and here, in an uncertain year between 462 and 502, St David was born. Tradition has it that the birth was during a thunderstorm though the birthplace 'shone with so serene a light that it glistened as though the sun was visible and

A natural arch seen from the Coastal Path

God had brought it in front of the clouds'. During the birth a well sprang up nearby, St Non's Well.

After the birth St Non went to Brittany and is buried at Dinan in a chapel dedicated to her. The chapel whose remains we see here is of unknown date, but probably thirteenth century. A fine brass from it, dated to the late fourteenth century, was one of the oldest and finest in Wales, but though illustrations of it exist the brass itself was lost in the nineteenth century.

St Non's Well was one of the most sacred in Wales and visited by most pilgrims to St David's. It has miraculous healing powers, and is claimed to be especially good for eye disorders and helping pregnant women. The traditional offering to the well was a pebble or pin – many were found during a rebuilding and re-dedication in 1951 – but the walker will notice that today's visitor favours a monetary gift.

Nearby St Non's House was built in 1929 and taken over in 1939 by the Passionist Fathers. It offers religious retreat and also training and renewal courses for people from all walks of life. The new chapel – to Our Lady and St Non – beside the fence was built in the thirties, though it used many stones from other sacred sites, including St Non's Chapel. The window behind the altar is a fine pre-Raphaelite rendering of St Non.

### (6) St David's

Were it not for the cathedral the city of St David's – in Welsh *Tyddewi*, David's House – would be a village. Indeed, so small is the city, and so well hidden the cathedral, that it would be possible for an unfamiliar visitor to drive through without ever realising that the patron saint of Wales' cathedral was a few yards away.

From the 'village green', The Pebbles – so named because formerly it was pebbled – leads to Porth-y-Twr, the Tower Gate, a thirteenth century gateway to Cathedral Close. The close, containing the cathedral and the Bishop's Palace, was completely walled, and much of the wall remains intact. Beyond the gateway the cathedral comes into view, a magnificently compact, central-towered building, superbly set in the deep Alun valley and backed by the impressive ruins of the Bishop's

St David's Cathedral

Palace. The cathedral is reached down a flight of stone steps known as the Thirty-Nine Articles.

Very little is known about St David: the date of his birth is not known to better than forty years and even the date of his death, traditionally on 1 March, is not known. As the son of a prince he would have received a good education and training as a priest. It is told that he was consecrated as a bishop in Jerusalem and the portable altar stone in the cathedral's south transept is said to have been a gift from the Patriarch. St David spoke at the Synod of Brefi when tradition has it that a white dove flew down on to his shoulder. This explains the frequent representation of the saint with a dove on his right shoulder.

The first cathedral on the site was destroyed, probably by Viking raiders, in 645 and successive raids destroyed further buildings through to the eleventh century. Following the Norman conquest the area became more stable, and rebuilding work commenced in earnest, though it was not completed until the early sixteenth century. Progress was not helped by the collapse of the tower in 1220, a collapse that destroyed much of the completed work.

Tours of the cathedral are offered on Mondays in summer, and the interested visitor would do well to join one. Briefly, the building has a twelfth century core but much of the external work – in a curious purple sandstone – is fourteenth century. Inside, the cathedral is more elaborate, though very spacious and warm. The visitor will find the tomb of Edmund Tudor, father of Henry VII, whose remains were moved here from Carmarthen by his grandson, Henry VIII. Behind the high altar an excavated recess was found to contain a number of bones, assumed to be those of St David and St Justinian. Formerly these were in a reliquary that pilgrims could touch, but may have been hidden at the Reformation. They are now held in an oak casket.

The Bishop's Palace beside the cathedral is a magnificent building, both in position and construction. The palace is thirteenth and fourteenth century, but fell into disrepair after the Reformation, a decay hastened by the stripping of lead from the roof, the usual fate of monastic houses at the time. A tour of the palace, now in the hands of Cadw, the Welsh Heritage organisation, is well worth while, especially to see the wheel window in the eastern wall of the Great Hall, a superb feature.

## Walk 11 The Preseli Hills

The Pembrokeshire Coast National Park moves significantly inland only once, to enclose the Preseli Hills, old Pembrokeshire's only real upland mass. The hills are low by Welsh standards, barely making it to 500 m (1650 ft), though there is a large area of land above 300 m (1000 ft), and measure only about 16 km by 8 km (10 x 5 miles). Nevertheless the area is of the greatest interest to the prehistorian, not least because of its associations with Stonehenge, and offers a superb series of vantage points.

When man was first making his mark on the landscape of Britain, with his stone axe factories and cromlech burial chambers, some of the country's valleys would have been inhospitable places, a land of wild boar and wolves. If a high ridge was bare of trees then that would be the place to walk, and it is believed that the east-west ridge of Preseli was crossed by an ancient track. The local axe factories –there are known to have been two from an analysis of the micro-structure of the rock, and though their exact locations have not been discovered it is probable that one lay near Carn Menyn – exported their work to County Antrim and to 'Wessex', approximately due west and due east. The ridge trackway has long been known and has been given a variety of names by people anxious to explain away its origin. It was the Roman Road, though that it almost certainly was not; it was the Robbers' Road, a name given, perhaps, when times had changed and the valleys were more hospitable than the high land; and it was the Flemings' Way, improbable and more likely to be explained by the thoughts of the locals on those alien settlers.

In fact the proliferation of ancient burial sites almost certainly gives the age. There are neolithic cromlechs most famously at Pentre Ifan, on the northern flank of the hills – standing stones – and alignments and there are Bronze Age burial sites by the score. As with all later peoples, these early Pembrokeshire dwellers raised their churches and buried their dead beside the road.

The walk along the Preseli ridge is a fine one, especially in spring when the gorse and heather combine to form a carpet of yellow and purple, but the knowledge that you are following a trail that is, perhaps, 5000 years old adds to the attraction.

*Walk Category* : Difficult (4 hours).

*Length* : 16 km (10 miles) for a single traverse of the length of the ridge.

*Ascent* : 350 m (1150 ft).

*Maps* : Landranger Sheet 145; Pathfinder Sheet SN03113 (Newport (Trefdraeth) and Eglwyswrw).

*Starting and finishing point:* Unfortunately the Preseli Hills form a single east-west ridge a traverse of which leaves the walker a long way from his start point. The easiest way to overcome this is by the use of two cars parked one at each end of the ridge. There are pull-ins at 075 322 near Bwlch Gwynt, and also at 165 331 at the ridge's eastern end. Alternatively, a car can be left at Bwlch Gwynt, the walk can be completed and a bus taken from Crymych to Narberth where another can be used to regain Bwlch Gwynt.. This is not a satisfactory arrangement as the buses are infrequent, but presents the only real alternative for the single-car walker who does not wish to double the stated distance. In fact, if the ascent of Foel Eryr and Foel Drygarn are omitted, the walker going only from Bwlch Gwynt to Carn Menyn and back, the total length is about the same, i.e. 16 km (10 miles).

From Bwlch Gwynt follow the obvious, and broad, track to the summit of Foel Eryr, the low peak to the west of the road (see (1) Foel Eryr). Retrace the path to the Bwlch and now go east heading towards, then following, the northern edge of the Pantmaenog Forest. Beyond the forest some walkers may wish to head south to climb Foel Cwmcerwyn, at 536 m (1760 ft) the highest point on the Preseli Hills. It is topped by four Bronze Age burial cairns – the excavation of one of which revealed the remains of a cremation and a fine urn – but it is a disappointing viewpoint, the forest interfering with much of the view over 180 degrees of the panorama. Better is to continue eastward where good and indifferent tracks can be followed or ignored to reach Foel Feddau. This low summit, 467 m (1530 ft) high,is also topped by a Bronze Age burial cairn.

Eastward again the track is followed past Cerrigmarchogion (see (2) Bedd Arthur) and on to Mynydd Bach. East again there is a shallow pass before the track rises to pass between Carn Bica and Carn Siân to reach Bedd Arthur (see (2) Bedd Arthur). Ahead now the stony mass of Carn Menyn beckons, though the ridge walk takes a curving line northward rather than dropping into the valley of the Afon Tewgyll. Soon the flank of Carn Menyn is reached, and though the track itself does not visit the top there will be few walkers who will escape the lure of this most extraordinary of places (see (3) Carn Menyn).

Relocate the track and continue eastward: the edge of a forestry plantation is soon reached. There is a small rise, and from the top of it the walker should leave the track north-eastward, heading directly for Foel Drygarn. This variant goes past Carn Ferched, the Daughter's Grave, an obscurely named Bronze Age barrow. From Foel Drygarn's summit (see (4) Foel Drygarn) go east to a track that heads downhill to reach our earlier track at a gate. Go through and turn right down a track to the road. For Crymych go left here, then right at the Y-junction to reach the A478. Go left for Crymych (see (5) Crymych).

(1) *Foel Eryr*

The 'mountain of the eagle' is 468 m (1535 ft) high, low enough to be insignificant in the list of Welsh peaks, but its position means that the view from it is remarkable. Perhaps the name derives from this eagle's-eye view, the panorama extending north to Snowdonia, east to Mynydd Ddu, the first sandstone block of the Brecon Beacons National Park, south to Exmoor's Dunkery Beacon and westward across the Celtic Sea to the Wicklow Mountains. All on a clear day of course. More locally the view takes in virtually the whole of the new county – but old kingdom – of Dyfed. Indeed, so good is the panorama that it has been suggested that in prehistory the reason for Preseli's sacred nature was a belief that it represented the 'navel of the world', the centre of the local people's known universe.

425m

450m
CAIRN
*

400m

⑤

425m

425m

400m

FOEL
ERYR
(468m) ①

400m

BWLCH
GWYNT

↑↑↑↑↑    ↑↑↑↑↑↑

4

500

CRAIG
Y CWN

550m
▲

FOEL CWMCERWYN
(536m)

FOEL DRYGARN ④
(363m)

CAIRN

350m *▲

275

325m

325m

325m

325m

CARN
DAFADD-LAS
▢

325m

300m

350m
BEDD ARTHUR

375m

CARN · MENYN
③

CARN
FERCHED

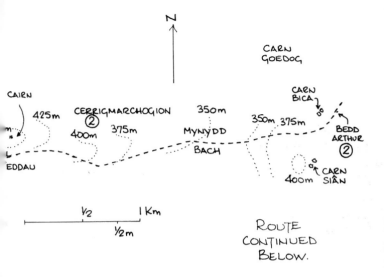

N

CARN
GOEDOG

CAIRN

CARN
BICA

425m

CERRIGMARCHOGION

350m

350m 375m

②

BEDD
ARTHUR

400m

375m

MYNYDD

②

EDDAU

BACH

CARN
SIÂN

400m

½         1 Km

½ m

ROUTE
CONTINUED
BELOW.

CRYMCH

Westward from Foed Eryr the ancient walkers had to follow the beautiful Gwaun valley to reach Fishguard, one postulated harbour for Irish traders. Curving south (left) the track could have used Mynydd Cilciffeth – itself topped by Bronze Age cairns – arriving in the valley near Llanychaer – about 5 km (3 miles) from Fishguard. Alternatively – and more probably – going north, the track reached Carn Ingli, topped by a large, but later, hill fort as well as numerous cairns, Mynydd Dinas (more cairns), Carn Slani and Carn Fran.

(2) *Bedd Arthur*

This oval of twelve stones, at 131 325, is claimed to mark the grave of King Arthur. The dedication is hardly unique and indeed there is another site, Carn Arthur – where one boulder is perched on another, at 135 323 a few hundred metres to the south-east, though off the ridgeway, which is also claimed as the grave site. It is not unusual to find prehistoric sites associated with ancient gods and heroes, especially if the sites include megaliths. Clearly these huge standing stones could only have been raised by superhuman efforts. Arthur was the obvious superhuman, especially for a Celtic people who had been harried for centuries, first by Saxons and then by Normans, and were in need of supernatural help. In addition to the two named sites, Cerrigmarchogion – at 111 323, earlier on the ridgeway – is the Stone of the Knights, and Cerrig Meibion Arthur – at 118 310, to the south of the ridgeway – are two upright stones, the Sons of Arthur.

The Preseli Hills also form the backdrop for some of the tales in *the Mabinogion*. One story has Arthur carrying out numerous 'impossible' deeds in order to win Culhwch his bride, the giant's daughter Olwen. One task is to take a comb and shears from the head of Twrch Trywyth, the giant magic boar whose landing place we saw on Walk 10 (see Note (4) of Walk 10). Arthur and his men hunted the boar from the coast to Preseli where, after a chase over the ridge, it turned and fought near Foel Cwmcerwyn, mentioned early in the walk. The boar killed four knights, but was hunted on to the Severn where the comb was captured. The hunting of the boar also crossed Mynydd Ddu, where a river is named for the magic beast (see Note (1) of Walk 15).

Carn Menyn

In addition to Arthurian stories, many of the sites on Preseli have associated folk-tales. Carn Goedog, at 129 332, is the burial site of the black pig in the Welsh ballad of that name – *Y-Mochyn Du*. Carn Siân – at 129 321, near Bedd Arthur – is said to have been the site of a chapel to St Silyn. But best of all is Carnedd Meibion Owen at 090 362, north of Bwlch Gwynt. This is named for the three sons of Owen who decided to fight for their father's land, even before he had died!, rather than divide it between them as the Welsh *gavelkind* required them to do. They made wooden clubs and fought all day on the hill, but as night fell no one had won. Eventually the father chose one son, sending the others to the kings of England and Scotland.

(3) *Carn Menyn*

In its most complete form Stonehenge consisted of a circle of large sarsen stones coupled by lintels, an inner ring of smaller, unlinteled stones, an outer horseshoe of five huge, paired, linteled sarsens and an inner horseshoe of nineteen smaller, unlinteled stones around a central 'altar' stone. In 1923 Dr. Herbert Thomas of the Geological Survey made the astonishing discovery that the inner circle and inner horseshoe stones were mostly of a spotted dolerite, known as bluestone, that forms the outcrops of Carn Menyn and Carn Ddafad-las here on the Preseli Hills' eastern end. Small numbers of stones were also found to be from nearby Foel Drygarn and Carn Alw, to the north of Carn Menyn. Various theories have been put forward to explain this discovery, which appears to belie the 'primitive'nature of Bronze Age folk and so beggared belief in the twenties, but the best of these, that a large number of stones had been 'accidentally' transported by ice during the last Ice Age, has now given way to the theory that the stones were transported by the Bronze Age Beàker Folk from Preseli to Milford Haven and floated to the mouth of the Bristol Avon. The stones were then floated upstream, hauled to the River Wylie, floated again, then finally hauled to the Stonehenge site.

Why? Salisbury Plain is littered, still, with sarsen stones of all sizes; there was no need to haul stones to it and certainly not from West Wales. Geoffrey of Monmouth, writing *The History of the Kings of Britain* in the early twelfth century, notes that Aurelius Ambrosius wished to raise a memorial over Celtic dead who had been killed by Hengist the Saxon.

Merlin suggests that a suitable memorial would be the transfer of the Giant's Ring, a stone circle, from Ireland to the burial site on Salisbury Plain. When Aurelius points out that Britain is not lacking in stones, Merlin counters by telling the king that the Giant's Ring stones have mystical powers. The king agrees and Merlin brings the stones, by sea and land. Hengist was a fifth century Saxon and Ireland is not Preseli, but Geoffrey could well have been picking up a folk memory that the bluestones were an ancient holy circle and were moved because of it. Preseli, indeed Wales, is short of stone circles. There is one, well set, but of small stones, that we shall see on Walk 17. Preseli has just one site, near Gors Fawr, at 134 294 to the south of Carn Menyn. That site has sixteen stones, each about 1 m (3 ft) tall, set in a not quite circular arrangement 20 m (66 ft) in diameter. However that Welsh shortage does not mean that there was not an important and large site on Preseli some 4000 years ago. England does not have a large number of stone circles either, but it does have Avebury and Stonehenge. It therefore seems likely that there was an important site on or near the Preseli Hills, and that it was moved to the then more important site on Salisbury Plain.

Cern Menyn would not have been a quarry in the modern sense. Rather it would have been a birthplace, large blocks of stone being naturally weathered by frost-cracking, from the outcrop. It is truly memorable to stand among the jumble of stones on the south side of Carn Menyn and to think that 4000 years ago men laboured to move similar stones so many miles.

(4) *Foel Drygarn*

Foel Drygarn, the hill of three cairns, is indeed crowned by three Bronze Age burial cairns, quite the largest of their kind in West Wales. Later, during the Iron Age, the hill was fortified, three ramparts being visible. All over the summit plateau, within and between the ramparts, hut circles have been found. Because of its position, Foel Drygarn offers a superb view of the ancient ridgeway, and is well worth leaving the track to climb.

(5) *Crymych*

Crymych itself is a straggling village with little to detain the walker. But to the east is a fine hill, Freni Fawr, a last outcrop of the Preseli Hills.

Another tale from the *Mabinogion* is set here, in which the Roman Emperor Magnus Maximus hunts on its flank and camps on its summit. In Welsh the Emperor's name is Macsen Wledig, which explains the occasional name given to the hill, Cadair Facsen. The hill is also topped by Bronze Age cairns and reputedly home to a pot of gold. Usually such pots are buried beneath a cairn, but here it is just somewhere on the hillside. As is also usual, the pot is guarded, here by a hurricane-inducing phantom.

## Walk 12 St Govan's Head (a) Castlemartin (b) Bosherston Lily Ponds

In the south of Pembrokeshire there are superb limestone cliffs all the way from Castlemartin to the outskirts of Tenby, and these are followed by the official Pembrokeshire Coastal Path. Though low by 'huge sea cliff' standards – the cliffs rarely exceed 40 m (130 ft), the limestone is in near-vertical sheets and occasionally sculpted into stacks, arches, caves and sharply indented bays. There is interest all along this section of the coast: Lydstep Haven is a fine beach; Manorbier Castle, birthplace of Gerald of Wales, is superb; Stackpole Head is a fine jutting point and beside it is the romantically named Mowingword. But we go to the west, to concentrate on the area between Castlemartin and Bosherston. The Castlemartin cliffs have the disadvantage of forming part of the army's artillery range, though this does mean that access is reduced, leaving the cliffs quiet in the central section. Since access to the Castlemartin cliff path is occasionally restricted by firing, an alternative is offered that visits the interesting lily ponds near Bosherston.

*Walk category* : (a) Easy ($1^1/_4$ hours from St Govan's to Stack Rocks); (b) Easy (2 hours).

*Length* : (a) 6 km ($3^3/_4$ miles) from St Govan's to Stack Rocks; (b) 8 km (5 miles).

*Ascent* : (a) Flat; (b) 60 m (200 ft).

*Maps* :  Landranger Sheet 158; Pathfinder Sheet 1124 (SR89/99)
          Castlemartin and St Govan's Head.

*Starting and finishing point* :  The starting point for each walk is the car-park near St Govan's Chapel, at 967 930.This is reached by continuing along the lane from the B4319 near St Petrox that goes through Bosherston. For Walk 12(a) use of this car-park doubles the stated mileage unless another vehicle is available at the Stack Rocks car-park, at 925 945, reached by another signed road off the B4329 near the Merrion army camp. There is no public transport between the two car-parks.

### (a) Castlemartin

If the artillery range is open there is a fine walk along the cliffs to Elegug Stacks and the Green Bridge of Wales. Sadly the permitted track does not allow continuous access to the cliff edge and is occasionally littered with unsightly debris. But with a little ingenuity and a decision to look the other way here and there, this is a fine walk. **Within the range please do not touch any metal or odd-looking objects. Please also be careful if you have children, not only because of range debris, but because the cliff edges are sudden and unprotected, and very, very steep.**

From the car park go across to visit St Govan's Chapel (see (1) St Govan's Chapel) before going over the stile to reach the westward-going track over the Castlemartin range (see (2) Castlemartin). Soon there is a deep-cut inlet, Stennis Ford, beyond which the even narrower and darker, and more impressive, Huntsman's Leap is reached (see (3) Huntsman's Leap). Beyond, the track wanders inland occasionally, though numerous unofficial but beaten paths lead to the cliffs. The walker has rock climbers to thank for some of these access paths, the same climbers being responsible for the iron bars deeply embedded in the cliff-edge turf. These bars, which can trip the unwary – and this is no place to trip – are for belaying and abseiling. A metalled road is reached over a stile, but this is soon left in favour of the track which cuts off the headland of The Castle (see (4) Flimston). Westward the track reaches

VIEWPOINT
GREEN
BRIDGE
OF WALES
⑥ₐ

FLIMSTON
CASTLE ④ₐ

ELEGUG
STACKS
⑤ₐ

BULLSLAUGHTER
BAY

MEWSFORD
POINT

N
↑

HILL FORT

BOSHERSTON ③b

LILY PONDS ②b

½    1 Km

½m

FOOTBRIDGE

CASTLEMARTIN RANGE

P

S

S

S

BROAD HAVEN ①b

STEPS

SAND LIMIT

M.O.D. BUILDING

S

G  S

NEW QUAY

Ⓢ

S

PATH BESIDE MARKER POSTS.

HUNTSMAN'S LEAP

STENNIS FORD

ST. GOVAN'S CHAPEL

①a

STEPS

ST. GOVAN'S HEAD

LOOKOUT

the oddly named Bullslaughter Bay, and at the bay's eastern end the view really opens out. The Elegug Stacks and Green Bridge come into view, in the distance, while close to hand the folded rocks and caves of the bay's cliffs are superb. Beyond the bay the track is away from the cliff until Flimston is reached (see also (4) Flimston). This astonishing headland can be viewed at very close quarters, but do take great care, the cliffs are sheer and unprotected and on the seaward side of The Cauldron the land bridge between sea and sea-filled hole is narrow. Beyond Flimston are the Elegug Stacks (see (5) Elegug Stacks) and the Green Bridge (see (6) Green Bridge of Wales) which is equipped with a viewing platform on its western side.

If no car awaits the walker at the Stack Rocks car-park, then the whole experience can be enjoyed again immediately, from the opposite direction.

## (1) *St Govan's Chapel*

St Govan's Chapel is reached by a stone stairway. If you count the steps as you descend and then again on the way up, tradition says that you will not arrive at the same number.    The chapel is named for Gobhan or Govan, sixth century abbot of Dairinis in Wexford, Ireland, who landed here having sailed across the Celtic Sea in his coracle. His hermitage cell was formed by cutting into the rock, and this cell can still be reached from the chapel built, of local stone, by his followers. The cleft in the cell's rock wall is said to have hidden Govan when raiders landed nearby. If the visitor enters the cleft he can make a wish. The now empty bell-cote once held a silver bell which was stolen by raiders whose ship was wrecked on their escape. Sea nymphs rescued the bell and returned it to the site, but to protect it against further raids they placed it in the middle of a rock near the well. If you find the right rock the bell will ring when you strike it. The well is seaward of the chapel and is probably original. Now it is blocked by stones, but once it was revered for its healing powers.

An interesting tradition links the chapel to Arthurian legend. The lake at Bosherston is one of many that claim to be that into which Bedivere

The Green Bridge of Wales

threw Excalibur, while Govan is said to derive from Gawaine, having been the final home of that knight after Arthur's last battle.

## (2) *Castlemartin*

The Castlemartin range is one of the largest in Wales and is used for the firing of live ammunition. The merits or otherwise of such ranges need not be discussed here, but the choice of Castlemartin does have a link with history, the Castlemartin Yeomanry being the only regiment to have been awarded a battle honour for a battle on British soil. In 1797 1400 Frenchmen – half of them reluctant conscripts, and led by a British-hating American – landed at Carregwastad Point near Fishguard. They captured a farm, got drunk on stolen liquor, were frightened to death by the sight of the Fishguard women-folk who, because of their red cloaks and tall hats, they thought were Guardsmen, and surrendered to the Yeomanry with little resistance on the following day.

## (3) *Huntsman's Leap*

This narrow cleft has also been called Adam's Leap, but the more common name derives from a local tale that a rider being pursued along the cliff by robbers or creditors jumped the chasm to escape them. He stopped and dismounted to see what he had crossed and died of fright.

## (4) *Flimston*

On this section of the coast there are two promontory forts. The Castle is the earlier, dating from around the second century. Below it, at low tide, the boilers of the *Ionian*, a wrecked World War 1 troopship, can be seen.

Flimston Castle is later, dating from the fourth century, though the name is later still, deriving from 'Flemish town' because tradition has the Flemish settlers arriving here in the early twelfth century. The Cauldron, the most obvious feature, is a huge hole produced by limestone folding and erosion. The sea pounds into the hole through a natural arch that can be crossed, and offers a spectacular view of nature in the raw.

## (5) *Elegug Stacks*

The stacks are named for an ancient, seemingly non-Welsh, word for guillemot, an apt name in view of the number of the auks that nest on them. The bigger stack is Elegug Tower, the smaller, more elegant one is

Elegug Tower

Elegug Spire. Each can be climbed – out of the auk-nesting season – by routes at about VS (Very Severe) grade. The descent, from indifferent abseil anchors, is awesome. In addition to guillemots there is a large breeding population of razorbills and fulmars.

### (6) *Green Bridge of Wales*

In the evolution of the coast by marine erosion caves in the cliff are the earliest sign. If the rock formations are appropriate, two back-to-back caves form a natural arch which eventually collapses to leave sea stacks. Locally there are fine examples of the process. Flimston has one robust, early arch, while the Elegug Stacks are the remains of one or more arches. The Green Bridge is a superb, slender midway point. Soon, on a geological timescale, the arch will collapse to leave a single stack. The Green Bridge can be crossed, but crossers should be cautious. It is narrow and precarious and in high winds downright dangerous.

### (b) Bosherston Lily Ponds

If the Castlemartin range is closed this walk offers a fine alternative. In its early stages it crosses another part of the range, but one that is more frequently open. Even if it is closed Bosherston village can be reached and used as a car-park so that the lily ponds and Broad Haven can be reached.

From the car-park visit St Govan's Chapel (see Note (1) of Walk 12(a)). From the top of the chapel steps take the metalled track that follows the cliff edge closely to the coastguard look-out at the southern tip of St Govan's Head. This cliff area is favoured by climbers so please be careful to avoid the iron bars banged into the cliff-edge turf to act as belay and abseil points. The path must now be retraced, for two reasons, firstly as the official coastal path is the only right of way, and secondly to avoid the deep incut from the old harbour of New Quay.

The official path is marked by white posts to another car-park at 975 939 where steps lead down right to the beach of Broad Haven (see (1) Broad Haven). Cross the back of the beach, heading almost due north, to where the stream runs on to it. Follow the stream to where a three-way sign offers the choice of coastal path out and back, and Bosherston. Take the last, keeping the lake on your left hand. The lake (see (2) Bosherston

Lily Ponds) is crossed by a grassy bridge. At its end go left to reach a stone causeway that crosses the lake again. From the causeway a path leads to another causeway that crosses the lake for a third time. Between the causeways there is an inaccessible Iron Age fort on the hill to the right on a spur of land between the lake arms.

From the end of the last causeway a path leads easily up to a car-park beside Bosherston church. Go along the lane to the village road (see (3) Bosherston). There turn left and follow the road back to the start.

### (1) *Broad Haven*

The St Govan's Broad Haven is occasionally referred to as Broad Haven South to avoid confusion with the other beach of the same name near St. Bride's. The name Stackpole, applied to the nearby headland, the extensive dune system to the east of the ponds and the estate on which the ponds lie, is believed to be Norse in origin, probably from *stac*, a rock pillar – those in the bay, no doubt – and *poler* , an inlet. The dunes at the back of the haven have grown since the damming of the ponds at the end of the eighteenth century and their ecology is fragile. Please be careful not to destroy either the plant life or the dunes themselves. The dunes are held together by marram grass, but there are lovely little patches of colour in summer, the blue viper's bugloss and the pink restharrow. Overshadowing some of the flowers is sea buckthorn, a tallish, fast-growing shrub with a mixed reputation. Its berries help feed migrating birds, its sharp thorns deter people and so protect the dunes, but it does suffocate lower, less hardy species.

### (2) *Bosherston Lily Ponds*

The Stackpole Estate was owned by the Scottish Earls of Cawdor until it was transferred to the National Trust, and it was members of this family who dammed the valleys of three streams bound for Broad Haven to form the lily ponds. The ponds cover 32 hectares (80 acres) and are nationally important because of the underlying calcareous marls. The lakes hold perch, roach, tench and pike – as well as Excalibur, see Note (1) of Walk 12(a) – while the surface is often criss-crossed by dragonflies. The ponds are famous for their lilies, which are at their best in June. The ponds are popular with birds, especially heron, coot, moorhen, swans and mallard.The lucky visitor will see the electric blue flash of a kingfisher, while in winter there is a good collection of winter migrants. Over twenty species of duck have been recorded, including goosander, smew and goldeneye.

### (3) *Bosherston*

Bosherston is a tiny village: a few houses, a pub, a tea-shop and the church of St. Michael and All Angels. The church is thirteenth century Norman, and has a fine stained glass window of St Govan. It also has a good hagioscope or squint, a passage in the chancel wall that allowed those in the side chapel to see the altar. Outside is an old cross, perhaps as old as the church itself.

St Govan's Chapel

# The Gower Peninsula

To the west of Swansea is an oblong block of land measuring about 25 km by 14 km (15 by 8 miles) that appears to have been tacked on almost as an afterthought. The Gower Peninsula is a land of scenic contrasts. To the south there are superb limestone sea cliffs, as well sculpted as any to be found in the southern part of the Pembrokeshire Coast National Park, while to the north there are broad sand and mud flats on the edge of the Burry estuary. Linking the two in the west is Rhosili Bay, with one of the finest stretches of flat sand in Wales, enclosed by the interesting horns of Worm's Head and Burry Holmes. Inland the Gower is flat pastoral land with few raised sections. Indeed the best 'upland' area is Rhosili Down which backs the sand of Rhosili Bay.

Gower – the locals will quickly tell you that you can say The Gower Peninsula or Gower, but that you must never, ever say The Gower – was a strange land. Heavily 'Normanised' in the early years after the conquest, the peninsula was always less Welsh than the surrounding land, the locals an island race proud of their independence, which they guarded jealously. The sea coast, particularly the jagged rocks of the south and Rhosili Bay, were notoriously dangerous in the days of sail: in places the ghosts of wrecked and drowned mariners must stand shoulder to shoulder on the cliff tops. Some of the wrecks – and I do not exaggerate the numbers, whole books have been written on Gower shipwrecks – were 'assisted' by false lights, though it must also be said that many of the locals were as brave in their assistance of sailors in distress as others were keen on helping cause the distress.

Of late, Gower has seen a revival of its fortunes as a holidaying centre, but its roads are too narrow, its bays too small and too difficult to reach for it ever to suffer from overburdening hordes. It is to be hoped that its cliffs will long remain the haunt of the fulmar, that most marvellous of all fliers, and the interested walker.

## Walk 13 Rhosili

At the extreme south-western tip of the Gower Peninsula there is an excellent diversity of scenery in a small area: open downland, a huge sandy beach, limestone caves, and an extraordinary geological feature. Our walk visits all of these. Rhosili, because of its position, is windswept, but our walk traverses from south-facing to west-facing cliffs and so guarantees some shelter if there is a steady blow. Rhosili – that is the now preferred spelling of a name that has more variations in its spelling than it has letters – has always been popular with the tourist. Dylan Thomas, a man of nearby Swansea, wrote a famous short story, 'Who do you wish was with us?', about a visit here, a story still as true now as when he wrote it.

The walker on this route can visit Worm's Head if he wishes, but should bear in mind that the 'causeway' to the Head is only open for $2^1/_2$ hours each side of low tide. Check the times for crossing on the notice-board of the National Trust shop near the car-park.

*Walk Category* : Intermediate ($3^1/_2$ hours) if Worm's Head is visited.

*Length* : 9 km ($5^1/_2$ miles).

*Ascent* : 200 m (650 feet).

*Maps* : Landranger Sheet 159; Pathfinder Sheet 1145 (SS 48/58/68) South Gower and the Mumbles.

*Starting and finishing point* : The car-park at the western (far) end of Rhosili village, reached by taking the B4247 that leaves the A4118 Swansea to Port Eynon road at the village of Scurlage.

From the car-park go first to the National Trust shop to check the access times to Worm's Head. Now go back along the village road to Devon View where a lane goes right. Take this and bear left at a Y-junction. The lane is soon unfenced on the right, and when the fence returns there is another Y-junction with the right arm blocked by a gate, to the side of which is a stile. Go over the stile. Ahead now there is a difficulty. Across the field there is a half-stile and beyond, an avenued track to a lane. But the avenued track has been blocked in the most flagrant way. The real problem seems to be a camping site across the field and to the

# WALK 13  RHOSILI

N

RHOSILI

BAY

WORM'S HEAD ②

OUTER
HEAD

MIDDLE
HEAD

INNER
HEAD

½    1Km

½m

LOW TIDE
LIMIT

SAND LIMIT →

SWEYNE'S HOWES

RHOSILI BEACH ③

RHOSILI DOWN ⑤

175m

CAIRNS

THE BEACON (193m)

175m

150m

125m

KG

75m

100m

⑤

RHOSILI ④

G

N.T. SHOP

75m

LADDER

G

S

S

50m

S

①

S

TOR'S
TRE

left. Campers seem to be using the avenue as a makeshift toilet and have incurred – hardly surprisingly – the wrath of the landowner, who has attempted to prevent access.

Custom seems to take the walker right from the stile, along the field edge to a half-stile on to a track that is the public footpath. Go right and follow this track over three stiles to open cliff. The fields this track crosses, and those to the right, are a fascinating reminder of an ancient way of agriculture (see (1) Rhosili field system). Beyond the last stile the path reaches a stepped wall descended by a ladder at an awkward angle. Ahead now are two paths, both reaching the same point eventually. The upper has the advantage of losing no height, while the lower is exciting, taking the crumbling cliff edge above Fall Bay to reach rock slabs on the far bay side. If the lower path is taken there is another choice at the slabs, one path going along the back of the slabs and staying at shore level until the point is reached, the other rising to reach the first upper path near a wall of the old field system. Along either path the walker stands every chance of being entertained by the famous nursery-rhyme call of the yellow-hammer.

The upper path follows the old wall at first, then goes ahead as the wall goes right, to reach a building that was once a coastguard look-out, but is now a nature reserve visitor centre. From here, a descent can be made to the shore. This is worth-while even if the land bridge to Worm's Head is flooded as the rock pools abound with life. Hermit crabs are especially numerous here. If tides permit the crossing can be made to Worm's Head (see (2) Worm's Head). Do be cautious: there is no path, the way is laborious and over slippery and jagged rocks on which it is easy to slip. The author once witnessed a helicopter rescue from the causeway's centre, the winchman just beating the tide to a visitor who had broken an ankle sliding off a patch of seaweed. The Worm is in three parts, a path taking the left-hand side of Inner Head to reach the Middle and Outer Heads.

From the old look-out a return to Rhosili is easily made along the broad cliff-top path. The view of the cliffs, from which limestone  was quarried and also burnt in local kilns, and of the broad sweep of Rhosili Beach (see (3) Rhosili Beach) is superb. Having regained the car-park continue into the village, passing the bus stop to the left, beyond which is a lane going round the left side of the church (see (4) Rhosili church). Where the lane emerges go left and down a lane to a kissing gate that gives access to Rhosili Down. Climb to the Down's trig point and continue a little way along the ridge to visit Sweyne's Howes (see (5) Rhosili Down). Retrace the route to the start.

(1) *Rhosili field system*

A look at the Pathfinder map of South Gower reveals an astonishing network of field boundaries near Rhosili. This area, known as the Viel or Vile, is good limestone farmland, in contrast to the poor, acidic Old Red Sandstone of the Down, and was divided into strips by low grass banks. Village folk were allocated strips at random to ensure a mix of good and bad land, and as later fences and walls were placed along the grass banks – which can still be seen – the old field pattern remains, one of the best survivals of a medieval field system in Britain.

(2) *Worm's Head*

The name 'worm' is Old English, often taking the form 'orm', and means a dragon or, more likely in this case, a sea serpent. The Head is an outlier of harder rock, an eccentric form of the sea stacks we met on Walk 12(a). In form it is two rock masses, the long, tent-shaped Inner Head being joined by a long ridge of rock and a rock arch – known as the Devil's Bridge – to a second mass. This second mass is half divided by a thinned section into the Middle and Outer Heads. On Outer Head there is a blow hole, air being compressed in a lower sea cave and puffed piston-like out of a vertical fissure. Outer Head is a noted bird sanctuary, especially for razorbills, guillemots, kittiwakes and fulmars, and climbing on it, indeed access to it, is prohibited from 1 March to 31 July each year.

Not surprisingly the Head has attracted local tales. One such is that the Celtic saint Cenydd – after whom Llangennydd, at the northern end of Rhosili Down, is named – set adrift as a child, on the sea in a wicker cradle, was rescued on to the Worm by seabirds. Leland, the Elizabethan traveller, was convinced that the Worm was a magical doorway to another world, claiming that there was a 'Hole at the Poynt of Worme Heade, but few dare enter it, and Men fable there that a Dore within the spatius Hole hathe be seen with great nayles in it'. Leland also claimed that there was a secret passageway beneath the sea from the Head to a place in Carmarthenshire.

On a calm, sunny day the Worm is a friendly place, but with a stormy sea running it seems far from hospitable, yet there is evidence of a hill fort on Inner Head, and bones found in a cave on Outer Head suggest a mesolithic presence.

## (3) Rhosili Beach

Between Worm's Head and Burry Holm there is an 8 km (5 mile) arc of beautiful sand, one of the finest of Welsh beaches. But in the days of sailing ships Rhosili Bay could often be a far from happy place. Facing due west it could be an unavoidable target for a windblown ship, and many have come to grief. The most famous is the least well documented. In the later part of the seventeenth century a gold-landed Spanish galleon came ashore, though nothing definite about the ship, its crew or its position is known. A very low tide in 1807, and another in 1823, allowed a large number of silver dollars to be found far out towards the sea but on each occasion the incoming tide prevented an exact position of the hoard to be marked. Today the 'Dollar Ship' is another treasure trove awaiting its lucky finder.

More obvious are the timbers of the *Helvetia* that can be seen at the southern end of the bay. The timbers are all that remain of a barque that grounded in November 1887. Luckily all the crew escaped unharmed, though five men were sadly lost when a salvage ship was retrieving the *Helvetia's* cargo of wood.

## (4) Rhosili church

The church of St Mary the Virgin, though built in the fourteenth century, is Rhosili's second church, the first lying beneath the sands of The Warren, below the village. That first church, revealed in great detail by severe floods in 1979/80 was built in the mid-twelfth century. The present church is a stout Norman construction, notable for a memorial to P.O. Edgar Evans, a local man, who died with Scott on the retreat from the South Pole in early 1912. Evans was a man of immense strength and was chosen for that reason, but he became exhausted by sledge-hauling and on 17 February became the first of the five-man team to die.

Fall Bay

## (5) *Rhosili Down*

On a good day, one with a reasonable inshore wind, the top of the Down and the sky all around is filled with hang-gliders, Rhosili being one of the country's foremost areas for the sport. At 193 m (632 ft) the Down offers sufficient height, and its sea face deflects the wind to give excellent up-draughts. The Down's summit, known as The Beacon, offers a superb panorama stretching from St Govan's Head in Pembrokeshire to Devon's Hartland Point. The summit area contains no fewer than founrteen Bronze Age burial cairns erected, it is believed, by the Beaker Folk who moved Preseli bluestones to Stonehenge.

The Sweyne's Howes, or Swine Houses, about a kilometre ($^1/_2$ mile) north of The Beacon, are older. Though having a Norse name they are in fact neolithic burial chambers – cromlechs – of a basic design. They are, perhaps, 1000 years older than the cairns which are themselves 3500 years old. There are two houses about 100 m apart.

Worm's Head

# The Brecon Beacons National Park

The Brecon Beacons National Park was designated by the National Parks Commission in 1957. It is huge, a total of 1330 square km (519 square miles) with land in four of the new Welsh mega-counties, Dyfed, Gwent, Mid-Glamorgan and – with almost two-thirds of the Park's area – Powys. Most people, when considering the Park, remember only the Old Red Sandstone masses. In one sense that is hardly surprising since the four distinct masses of Mynydd Ddu, Forest Fawr, the Beacons themselves, and the Black Mountains are the Park's most distinctive features and represent a sizeable proportion of its area.

But there is other and varied scenery within the Park's boundaries. To the south of Forest Fawr the limestone sheet that once capped the whole of the Old Red Sandstone still exists. This low-lying area is cave country, the sculpted limestone also producing waterfalls. The whole is enclosed in a typically lush limestone vegetation, the trees being especially good. Eastwards there is another area where the original limestone capping sheet is still present. At Llangattock, however, the limestone forms a high and exposed plateau which, while still being very good for caves, offers little chance for vegetation. Only where there have been quarries is there such plant life, as the old, steep quarry walls offer some protection.

Between the limestone of Llangattock and the sandstone block of the Beacons and the final, easternmost sandstone block of the Black Mountains runs the river Usk in its wide, gentle valley. The National Park is a generous shape with none of the exclusion zones of, say, the Snowdonia Park, or even the Pembrokeshire Coastal Park, and encloses the Usk from its source right through to Abergavenny. The valley is a good one, providing the best access to all areas of the Park and some secluded, if somewhat less easily accessed, river scenery.

In the walks that follow the main mountain masses are dealt with individually. Despite its wholeness in the geological sense the Park's masses are quite unique and, because of the Park's dimensions, quite well separated.

MYNYDD DDU

The most westerly of the sandstone masses of the National Park is also the biggest and, in a sense, the most poorly defined. There is a scarp slope, indeed the scarp slope is one of the steepest and most continuous in the Park, but it is set in the middle of a raised plateau and has not been weathered into distinctive peaks. As a result, the horns, as the angles of the scarp slope are called, though high, are not prominent summits as are, for instance, Corn Du and Pen y Fan.

Old Red Sandstone is a soft rock, as the weathered, well-rounded peaks indicate, and was easily sculpted by ice. Here the ice sheets scoured hollows at the bases of two of the steepest sections of scarp slope. In each case the glacial moraine created a dam when the ice retreated, trapping water to form corrie lakes. Llyn y Fan Fach lies at the foot of the northern scarp slope, a mysterious sheet of water, a home to fairies, while Llyn y Fan Fawr, the larger lake, as the name implies, but only just so, lies at the foot of the long eastern-facing scarp slope and is a friendlier stretch of water.

North of the scarp slope there is a raised plateau of land that has been forest-planted. Here the Usk rises from the Usk reservoir, the plateau ending where it meets the river's valley, and that of the Afon Gwyddarig that flows west to Llandovery. The real surprise lies south and west of the scarp slope, where the dip slope is an undulating plateau that extends over a huge area. This area, a tangled mass of shallow peaks and valleys, rock outcrops and bogs, is a true wilderness, the only real wilderness in the Park for all its high land. This moorland plateau is terminated by the Tawe valley, the river rising near Llyn y Fan Fawr and flowing close to a remnant of the limestone capping sheet. The sheet here is riddled with caves, to such an extent that it represents one of the finest caving areas in Britain.

## Walk 14 Carreg Cennen

At its extreme eastern edge Mynydd Ddu falls away into the Cennen valley, beyond which there is a rugged mass of limestone completely dominating the valley. This naturally defensive position was, not

surprisingly, exploited by the castle builders and today the gaunt ruins of
a thirteenth-century castle top the mass. Our route circles the mass,
gaining the best of the views of the castle, but also toward the edge of
Mynydd Ddu, close to an interesting historical site.

*Walk category* : Easy/Intermediate  ($2^1/_2$ hours).

*Length* : 8 km (5 miles).

*Ascent* : 250 m (800 ft).

*Maps* :  Landranger Sheet 159; Outdoor Leisure Sheet 12 Brecon
           Beacons National Park Western Area.

*Starting and finishing point*  : The castle car-park at  668 194, reached
by a minor, signed, road from the hamlet of Trapp, itself reached by
minor roads from the main A483 Llandeilo to Ammanford road.

From the car-park go back along the lane towards Trapp, and take the
lane to the left after about 150 m. This lane drops steeply between fine
hedgerows. When a house comes into view – Pantyffynnont, to the right
– look for a stile in the hedge to the right: it is waymarked, as is the
whole route, though occasionally not too well. Go over and steeply
down the field on an obvious, but indistinct, path to a second stile.
Beyond this the grass is even steeper and more slippery to another stile.
Go over to reach a double-stiled footbridge across the Afon Cennen. Go
half left and up to a half-stile, beyond which the going is steeply uphill
towards the buildings of Llwyn-bedw. Aim for the right-hand side of the
buildings and go right along the unfenced farm lane.
   The lane passes superb oak trees, crosses a cattle grid and ford and
then goes round a hairpin bend. Over another cattle grid a stile to the left
is reached. Go over and along the track, crossing a slab footbridge to
another stile. Beyond, the route leaves the stony track on a less distinct
path – the yellow marker on the last stile gives the direction – to another
stile. Beyond this the source of the Loughor can be reached on the right
(see (1) Source of the Loughor).

The way forward is the obvious stony track that becomes grassy and trends leftwards after a left-right swing. Beyond another stile the path becomes very indistinct: keep to the left of the obvious hollows, heading across the field to where the field's right retaining wall becomes a fence. There a stile leads to a minor road. Go left. To the right now is the final western edge of Mynydd Ddu. On its unfenced edge are a number of pillow mounds (see (2) Beddau'r Derwyddion).

Where the lane goes right, go left on a stony track – there is a waymarker here – to a stile. Ahead there is a distinct grass track to another stile beyond which the path becomes indistinct. Head to the right of the solitary hawthorn bush and go on to join a fence to the left. Ignore a stile on the left and go through a gate to a track. The track descends with many twists, going left where it joins another, to Hen-grofft farm, passing a number of superb sessile oaks. A gate gives access to the farmyard and another gives access to a lane beyond. While the journey across the farmyard is a right-of-way it does give me the odd feeling that I am intruding on someone's privacy. It is best to make haste, avoiding loitering and staring, and to ignore the farm dogs that may bark, but soon skulk away.

At the bottom of the farm lane go right and over a stile. Go across the field and up steps to another stile. Over the stile our route goes right, away from the castle. Leftwards the obvious path reaches beautiful woodland but soon becomes lost in an almost impenetrable mix of steep scree and low shrubs. The correct, rightward, path reaches the river and goes sharply up and left, continuing to the castle (see (3) Carreg Cennen Castle). Use the castle's approach path to regain the car-park.

## (1) *Source of the Loughor*
The river's source is reached over a stile and a fine makeshift bridge of fallen trees. The river rises from a cave, a tribute to the limestone country, and is a delight, even if the delight is moderated by the Welsh Water Authority sign which implies that unless told otherwise all visitors' natural reactions will be to pollute the water as much as they are able.

## (2) *Beddau'r Derwyddion*
The long and grassy mounds on the edge of Mynydd Ddu are known in Welsh as Beddau'r Derwyddion, the Graves of the Druids, and do indeed look like burial mounds. In fact they are artificial rabbit warrens, built by locals to act as a source of fresh meat when times were hard.

## (3) *Carreg Cennen Castle*
Carreg Cennen is such an obviously defensive feature that it is difficult to imagine that there has been a time when it has *not* been fortified. The first known occupation, however, is Roman, coins having been found on site that date their time here to the first to fourth centuries. Any later fortification by the Celts would have been obliterated by the stone-built castles, first mention of which is in 1248. At that time it was owned by

Carreg Cennen Castle

the local lord of Dinefwr, Rhys of Grufydd. That is an interesting ownership, especially to the visitor more used to the huge castles of North Wales, for it implies that Carreg Cennen was built by the Welsh, rather than by the Normans. Another interesting feature is that despite its apparent impregnability the castle changed hands no fewer than ten times in the ten years from 1277 to 1287 during disputes between local lords. A closer reading of the evidence from the feuds suggests that they were, in part, between the Welsh and the Normans and that Lord Rhys – Rhys's lordship was granted by Henry I – actually won the castle from a Norman owner and lost it to another. Certainly it was a Norman owner, Sir John Gifford, that remodelled the castle along the lines we see now. For a century the castle remained quiet, a quiet rudely shattered during the rebellion of Owain Glyndwr.

Glyndwr's rebellion was a vicious affair with each side breaking the unwritten rules of medieval warfare by looting monasteries and burning the land. Here at Carreg Cennen Glyndwr was asked by Sir John Scudamore, the castle's keeper, to grant safe passage to the womenfolk. Glyndwr refused and besieged the castle for months.

Later, during the Wars of the Roses, the Lancastrians used the castle, but surrendered it to a Yorkshire force after the battle of Mortimer's Cross in 1461. The Yorkists employed local labour, at a cost of £28, to dismantle the bulk of the defences, making the castle useless as a fortress and forming the ruin we see today.

One interesting feature of the ruin is the existence of a natural cave in the limestone beneath the castle, reached by a man-made passage through the rock. It does offer a source of water, though it was not the castle's sole source, and also, presumably, was a good cold storage room. It has also been suggested that the cave might have been 'included' in the castle design to prevent its use by an attacker. As there apears to be no access to it from outside this seems most unlikely. The visitor can borrow a torch to inspect the passage and cave.

## Walk 15 Deepest Mynydd Ddu

Behind the steep scarp slope of Mynydd Ddu the dip slope is a vast moor with swallet holes, bogs, streams and acres of good walking. The country is not easy to traverse, a place for the dedicated map and compass man, but deserves inclusion because on this alone of all the walks in the book the walker is likely to remain a solitary animal.

This walk is difficult and should only be attempted by the fit and those well versed in the use of map and compass. In very wet weather the conditions under foot can be atrocious and the route is not recommended at all if the visibility is poor.

*Walk Category* : Difficult (4 hours, for a one-way traverse).

*Length* : 14 km (9 miles) for a one-way traverse.

*Ascent* : 500 m (1650 ft).

*Maps* : Landranger Sheet 160; Outdoor Leisure Sheet 12 Brecon
Beacons Western Area.

*Starting and finishing point* : No reasonable round trip can be made from the walk, though it is possible to return around the scarp edge – more than doubling the stated distance. In the days of my youth a television quiz for families always had questions reserved for 'father and eldest child' and 'mother and youngest child'. This idea is appallingly sexist. In the case of this walk it could also be appallingly correct. The walker, alone or with senior sibling, should be dropped off north of Llanddeusant, rejoining the rest of the family for an outing to Dan-yr-Ogof caves. The start point is at 778 237 where there is a convenient dropping-off point beside the prominent 'No Parking' sign. This point is reached along a narrow lane that goes south from close to the church in Llanddeusant. The finishing point is the car-park below the entrance to the Dan-yr-Ogof caves, the first caves' car-park reached from the main A4067.

From the start point take the lane that goes north-east – the left fork of the Y-junction reached from Llanddeusant – and follow it through a gate and around a right-hand bend. A distinct, if tree-overhung, green path leaves this lane leftward, and this is the actual right-of-way. However it

soon becomes lost among undergrowth and fences, and it is better to
follow custom and practice, and to take a much more distinct track
leftward 100 m or so further on. This track is followed between fence
and hawthorn trees to a gate on to the open moor. There is no path ahead
now, the route going true south, then bearing slightly west to the top of
the obvious peak. There is a trig point on Carreg yr Ogof, and a shattered
limestone pavement that has created a mass of splintered stones and the
occasional 'wall' section. The limestone is delightful on this Old Red
Sandstone mass. I have yet to find the cave for which the peak is named.
It must be one of the few in Wales not named for Llywelyn or Owain
Glyndwr, and if that sounds cynical the Welsh have already retaliated by
writing 'English Go Home' on the trig point!

From Carreg yr Ogof the walker is on his own, the footpath marked
prominently on the maps being a good deal less prominent on the
ground. It is however best to follow its approximate line to pick up the
final track. Do not, therefore, go up Cefn y Carreg Las to the south –
although the ascent of this peak does allow the whole route to be
scanned, that not being possible from Carreg yr Ogof because of the
flank of the high horns (see Note (3) of Walk 17) – but descend south-
eastward on a bearing of 130°, continuing around the wide descending
flank of Bannau Sir Gaer to reach the Afon Twrch at 802 198. Cross the
river (see (1) Afon Twrch) and head for the top of the shallow peak of
Twyn Tal-Ddraenen, at 809 190, ahead. From the top continue south-
east to cross the Afon Giedd – named for Bwlch y Giedd, the pass
crossed by Walk 17 – to reach Pwll y Cig at 813 184. Beyond the Pwll a
more distinct track is followed south-east.

The track skirts the edge of Waun Fignen-felen, a bog of mystical
proportions that remains wet even in the driest of summers, for instance
1989, but is not the mother of rivers. Indeed the Afon Haffes forms the
eastern edge of the bog before running down Cwm Haffes. We go the
same way, passing the poorly defined hills (*twyns*) of Walter, Du and
Spratt. 'Du' is black, 'Walter' is interesting, but 'Spratt'? Beyond
Twyn Spratt the path joins a distinct, raised green lane that goes across
the hillside from right to left (south-west to north-east) at the boundary
of the Dan-yr-Ogof site. The site fence must not be crossed, but from it
there is a fine view of Craig-y-nos Castle (see (2) Craig-y-nos). Go left

instead, following the new track to the Afon Haffes which is crossed with a difficulty that depends entirely on the weather. In the valley below there are warning signs about the dangers of the river in flood. Go down the river's left bank to a gate in the wall, left, and follow the track beyond to and around the farm of Cerrig Haffes, to a gate on to the main road. Go right to reach the well-signed car-park at Dan-yr-Ogof (see (3) Dan-yr-Ogof).

(1) *Afon Twrch*

On Walk 10 we visited the landing spot in Wales of the magic boar Twrch Trywyth whose hunting is part of the story of Culhwch and Olwen in the *Mabinogion,* the book of Celtic legends. Culhwch, the hero of the story, is set a large number of seemingly impossible tasks by Olwen's father, a giant, including the obtaining of a comb and scissors from Twrch Trywyth's head for the giant to attend to his hair. Culhwch seeks King Arthur's help and Arthur agrees, explaining that the boar is a king turned into a pig for his sins. The boar comes ashore and is hunted across Preseli and Mynydd Ddu, and on to the Severn where the comb is obtained. The hunt then continues to Cornwall where the shears are finally won. Eventually all of the tasks are completed and Culhwch wins Olwen. The river here is named after the magic boar, a reminder of the chase across the moorland.

(2) *Craig-y-nos*

Craig-y-nos Castle was built in the grand style as recently as 1842 and was bought by the most famous opera singer of her day, Adeline Patti, in 1878. Madame Patti was born of Italian parents in Madrid in 1843 and when she came to Craig-y-nos she was at the height of a glittering career that took her all over the world. Craig-y-nos was her retreat, though countless distinguished guests visited it and she gave frequent performances of her greatest roles in the little theatre she had built within the castle. To these performances the local Welsh folk were often invited. In the grounds of the castle she created a pleasure ground, with an ornamental pond and an artificial lake complete with island. In 1898 her second husband died and the following year, at fifty-six, she married a twenty-nine-year-old baron, causing a local sensation. She died in 1919 and the castle was bought as a sanatorium. It later became a

WALKS 15 & 16 MYNYDD DDU

LLANDDEUSANT

S16

S15

250m

250m
300m
AVENUE
350m
400m
450m
500m
550m

G
G
G

NANT YR YSGWYDD

CARREG YR OGOF (585m)

550m
550m
55m

300m
350m
GAP
400m
WATER AUTHORITY BUILDING
WEIRS

450m
500m

LLYN Y FAN FACH

16.1

WALK 17

FAN FOEL (781m)

LLYN Y FAN FAWR

BANNAU BRYCHEINIOG (802m)

BANNAU SIR GAER (749m)

250m
CARREG
G. HAFFES
G.

200

300m

TWYN
SPRATT

TWYN
DU

450m

450m

350m

DAN-YR-OGOF
CAVES
(5,3)

CRAIC-Y-NOS
CASTLE
(5,2)

AFON HAFFES

TWYN WALTER

500m

PWLL Y CIG

500m

500m

TWYN
TAL-DDRAENEN

SWALLET
HOLES

500m

1 Km

½m

½

N ←

hospital for the elderly, but is currently 'between owners'.

The grounds now form the Craig-y-nos Country Park and are open daily all year.

(3) *Dan-yr-Ogof*

The Tawe valley near Craig-y-nos is now famous as a caving centre Ogof Ffynnon Ddu being one of the longest caves – and, to date, the deepest – in Britain, with nearly 50 km (30 miles) of explored passage. This cave lies to the east of the river. In 1912 two local brothers, the Morgans, discovered another cave on the western side, Dan-yr-Ogof. To date 14 km (9 miles) of this cave have been explored and the section open to the public is one of the finest, if not the finest, show cave in Britain. The extraordinarily beautiful features have names, but they are a good deal less fanciful than most. There is an underground pool, originally crossed by the Morgans in a coracle, and a fine waterfall. Best of all is The Cathedral, the largest chamber of any show cave in Britain and quite breathtaking. The cave complex includes reproductions of a neolithic burial  discovered here and of cave animals. Outside there is a 'zoo' of full-size dinosaurs, a little unconvincing for anyone over ten but forming part of a fine geological/geographical trail that can be thoroughly recommended. The site has a dry-ski slope, refreshments and a motel. It also has a seemingly endless supply of 'Do Not' notices. Are the visitors really so poorly behaved?

## Walk 16 Llyn y Fan Fach

Our second Mynydd Ddu walk reaches the smaller of the two Van lakes that nestle below the inverted tick of the Mynydd Ddu escarpment. It is a straightforward walk, a gentle introduction to the area, reaching a brooding stretch of water associated with one of the next remarkable folk-tales in Wales.

*Walk category* : Easy ($1^3/_4$ hours),

*Length* : 5 km (3 miles).

*Ascent* :  250 m  (800 ft).

*Maps* : Landranger Sheet 160; Outdoor Leisure Sheet 12 Brecon
Beacons Western Area.

*Starting and finishing point* : The village of Llanddeusant lies to the
north-west of the escarpment and is reached by narrow, but delightful,
country lanes from the north, the east and the west. For those
approaching from the west, several lanes reach the village from the
A4069 Brynamman to Llangadog road. From the north Llanddeusant can
be reached by an excellent but slow series of lanes from Llandovery
through Myddfai. The best approach is from the east, where a lane from
Trecastle, on the A40 Brecon to Llandovery road, reaches Pont ar
Hydfer and then, after a short forest section, crosses a high moorland
plateau that lies at the base of the escarpment before reaching
Llanddeusant. The view to the steep scarp slope is an appetiser for the
walk. From Llanddeusant a lane signed for the lake heads off eastward,
and this can be followed to a small 'car-park' that has been excavated
just short of the Water Authority sign which warns that no unauthorised
vehicles may pass the spot.

From the 'car-park' our route follows the Water Authority track
southward and uphill. The lucky walker here will see sandpipers which
are occasionally flushed out to disappear on swift, but shallow-beating,
wings, often piping as they go. There are also many meadow pippets
here and in spring the walker has a good view of their steep climbs and
parachuting descents as they stake their territorial claims. Near an
Authority building and a small complex of weirs the track is blocked by
a locked gate, but a gap in the wall, left, allows the gate to be bypassed
without the need for climbing. Continue to the lake (see (1) Llyn y Fan
Fach). To return to the start point the route is reversed. This sounds a
little unimaginative but our walk is a short one, and there are always fine
views – both local and distant – along the way.

## (1) *Llyn y Fan Fach*

Many years ago, a local young man called Rhiwallon regularly took his
lambs to the shores of the lake for pasture. On one trip he was astonished
to see a girl emerge from the water and sit on a rock at the lake's edge.

Rhiwallon fell in love with her immediately and offered her his lunchtime bread. She refused to take it, and refused unbaked bread the next time that Rhiwallon found her at the lake edge. Finally Rhiwallon's mother baked him a different sort of bread which the girl accepted. She agreed to Rhiwallon's offer of marriage but told the lad that he must first ask her father's permission and that she would leave him if he struck her three times. The next day Rhiwallon returned to the lake and was astonished to find the father there with six daughters, all identical. His love wiggled a toe so he could distinguish her when her father said Rhiwallon must be able to pick the right girl if he was to marry her, and the couple departed for their new life together.

Over the years three sons were born but Rhiwallon did strike her three times, each time just a tap to correct what he saw as incorrect behaviour – she laughed at a funeral and cried at a wedding – and on the third occasion she left him to return to the lake. She returned to visit her sons, to the oldest of whom, named Rhiwallon after his father, she taught her secret healing ways with herbs and other natural things. Rhiwallon, the son, became a famous local healer and passed the tradition on, giving rise to a line of local healers known as the Physicians of Myddfai, Myddfai being a small village a little way north of Llanddeusant.

On the face of it this is just another folk-tale, the legend of the Lady of the Lake, similar to many other local tales and, indeed, a few stories in the *Mabinogion*. However a delve into some of the odder features of some versions of the tale suggests a much more intriguing possibility. In some Rhiwallon and his family visit the lake girl's people – who are small and dark whereas his people are tall and blond – and their market, because there are many of them living in or sometimes on the lake. Rhiwallon cannot understand the girl's language and occasionally the unlucky strikes may not be with iron rather than not being with the hand.

When the tall, blond Celts came to Wales about 3000 years ago they encountered a Bronze Age people who were smaller and darker. They would not have been able to understand these people, and may have had difficulty in distinguishing them, after all, is it not true that all foreigners look alike? The Bronze Age people of Britain occasionally built their

Cefn y Carreg Las from Carreg yr Ogof

villages on rafts, as with the famous lake villages of Somerset, and to such a culture an iron sword or implement would have been a formidable, a fearsome thing, so fearsome perhaps that touching it would have been taboo. And the older culture might well have been skilled in herbal medicines to an extent that amazed the Celts. Bearing in mind all these ingredients – but bearing in mind also that what we are dealing with here is speculation not fact – then the tale could be a most remarkable folk memory of the meeting of two cultures. If that is so then the meeting would appear to have been a happy one, an intermixing rather than an annihilation, an opinion reinforced by a horde found in Glamorgan that contained both bronze and iron objects.

One thing that is certainly true is that there was a line of doctors from Myddfai. A quick investigation of the churchyard reveals a few, and it is known that from a Myddfai-born Aberystwyth doctor of the mid-nineteenth century an unbroken line goes back at least 600 years. In addition there is in existence a medieval book of remedies from the Physicians. It is full of homely (and good) advice on diet, even if some now seems dated – 'If thou desirest to die, eat cabbage in August'! Some of the remedies appear grimmer than the diseases they are meant to cure, for instance what could possibly be worse than taking a medicine made of chicken droppings, gunpowder and brimstone? To cure toothache a powder was made from ground-up newts and 'those nasty beetles which are found in ferns during summer' and applied to the tooth.

The folk tradition of the story has a peculiarly enduring nature. It is said that until very recent times local folk would visit the lake on the first Sunday of August to await the return of Rhiwallon's bride.

Taken together, the story of the Lady of the Lake and the Physicians of Myddfai offer one of the most intriguing legends to be found anywhere in Wales.

## Walk 17 The Horns of Mynydd Ddu

This walk visits the larger of the two Van lakes as well as reaching and following the scarp edge for an impressive view of Llyn y Fan Fach, the smaller lake visited on Walk 16. The walk also visits a small, but interesting megalithic site, one of a good number that exist on the eastern flank of Mynydd Ddu.

*Walk category* : Difficult ($4^1/_2$ hours).

*Length* : 14 km (9 miles).

*Ascent* :  750 m  (2500 ft).

*Maps* :  Landranger Sheet 160; Outdoor Leisure Sheet 12 Brecon Beacon
Western Area.

 *Starting and finishing point*  : At 852 215 on the minor road that links
the A4067 Ystradgynlais to Sennybridge road with Trecastle. This road,
going north from near the Dan-yr-Ogof caves, rises towards Bwlch
Cerrig Duon. Before reaching the summit of the pass there is a
prominent pull-off to the left of the road, overlooking the young River
Tawe.

From the start point follow the road southward to reach the megalithic
site of Cerrig Duon (see (1) Cerrig Duon) from which the road pass is
named. From the site the walker must cross rough moorland heading
north-westward towards Llyn y Fan Fawr. From the southern edge of the
lake a stream, Nant y Llyn, flows down to reach the Tawe. This stream
gives the line if it is reached, its left bank being followed all the way to
the lake outflow (see (2) Llyn y Fan Fawr).
   Cross the outflow and take the obvious rising path that crosses the
steep scarp slope to reach the skyline ridge at Bwlch y Giedd. The scarp
ridge here is impressive. Southward, its long sweep, known as Fan Hir –
the long crest – is a formidable barrier to the walker. As a digression it is
also a very fine walk, being reached from the Tawe valley, but further
south than our starting point. Northward, above Llyn y Fan Fawr, the
scarp slope is equally steep and formidable. It is no surprise that on this
little-walked block of the Brecon Beacons, where the walker is often
alone on the trackless moor,  a well-trodden route appears, to take him to
Bwlch Giedd.
   The climb to the depression in the Fan Hir ridge offers magnificent
views across the lake. At the Bwlch, go right (north) to climb to the
shelter and trig point of Bannau Brycheiniog (see (3) The Horns of

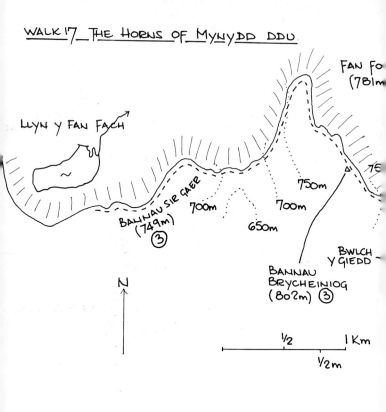

LLYN Y FAN FACH

FAN FO
(781m)

BANNAU SIR CAER
(749m)
③

700m

650m

700m

750m

75

Δ

N

BANNAU
BRYCHEINIOG
(802m) ③

BWLCH
Y GIEDD

½    1 Km

½m

Mynydd Ddu). Continue along the scarp edge to reach Fan Foel, from where the edge nips back on itself, turning south and then west to take the walker to Bannau Sir Gaer (see, also, Note (3)).

From Bannau Sir Gaer's summit it is worth continuing along the scarp edge to a point above Llyn y Fan Fach (see Note (1) of Walk 16). From there it is possible to take a well-marked path down the edge as it fades away westward to reach the smaller lake. From the lake it is then possible to cross the trackless moor at the base of the scarp slope all the way back to Llyn y Fan Fawr, reaching that lake's northern tip. This is the 'Best Walk', the scarp edge below Fan Foel, where it folds back on itself, being the most picturesque part of its length, and the untrodden moor being a wonderfully wild spot. It would, however, be understandable if some walkers preferred to reverse the outward route to Bannon Brycheiniog and Bwlch y Giedd, descending, then, the ascent route to Llyn y Fan Fawr.

From the lake's northern tip the source of the River Tawe can be reached. The river arises not from the lake, but from the moor a couple of hundred metres east of its north shore. In very wet weather the dry land gap between the two is tenuous, but in dry weather it is real enough. Despite the fact that Llyn y Fan Fawr is such a body of water and an obvious river source, only the small Nant y Llyn flows out of it As the walker follows the young Tawe downstream – and so returns to the starting point – he will notice that the moor to the east of the lake is, in fact, mother to many streams, the Tawe being a sizeable river long before the Nant y Llyn reaches it.

## (1) *Cerrig Duon*

There are few stone circles in Wales, and even fewer megalithic alignments, which makes Cerrig Duon – the Black Stones – an interesting site. The circle is about 17 m (55 ft) in diameter and consists of about twenty stones each 500–750 cm ($1^1/_2 - 2^1/_2$ ft) high. From the circle a short avenue of aligned stones leaves north-eastward towards the single, 2 m  ($6^1/_2$ ft) Maen Mawr – The Big Stone. That such alignments are rare in Wales makes the existence of another a few kilometres to the

Mynydd Ddu from the north

south a strange coincidence. That this second alignment – Saith Maen, the Seven Stones, at 852 154 – also points at Cerrig Duon is surely more than coincidence. Saith Maen consists, as the name tells us, of seven stones aligned along a straight line. The two largest stones, one 3 m (10 ft) and the other $2^1/_4$ m (7 ft) long, have fallen but the alignment of these and the others, each about $1^1/_2$ m (5 ft) high, is quite clear. It is believed that the megaliths, Cerrig Duon and Saith Maen, are Bronze Age, perhaps erected by the Beaker Folk who were also responsible for Stonehenge. That makes the sites 4000 years old, which represents an almost unbridgeable time gap. Did the alignments point out, signpost-like, a sacred route? Or was there some other purpose that we shall never grasp? We cannot know, but that does not detract from the power and mystery of the sites. Cerrig Duon is a wonderfully enigmatic, extraordinarily atmospheric, site.

Walkers of Walk 15 should note that Saith Maen is close to the Craig-y-nos Country Park, at the southern end of the route.

(2) *Llyn y Fan Fawr*

Llyn y Fan Fawr is a 'friendlier' stretch of water than its smaller neighbour, this being due in large part to its position on the sunny side of the hill. Assuming that the legend of Llyn y Fan Fach (see Note (1) of Walk 16) is just that, a legend, it is easy to see why that lake was chosen in preference to this, the larger one. On the scarp walls above the lake, where the sandstone is rich in lime, there is a fine collection of unusual plants, including mossy and burnet saxifrage, great burnet and roseroot. There are also fine outcrops of green spleenwort.

(3) *The Horns of Mynydd Ddu*

The names Bannau Brycheiniog and Bannau Sir Gaer mean, respectively, the Horns of Breconshire and the Horns of Carmarthenshire. Until the redrawing of county boundaries, the two peaks stood on either side of the boundary dividing the two old counties. Today the peaks still stand on either side of a county boundary though the boundary line that runs up the scarp slope to Fan Foel before heading south to follow the Afon Twrch, divides Dyfed and Powys. The name derives from the resemblance that the sharply turning scarp edge bears to

The summit of Bannau Brycheiniog

a horn, a resemblance that is vague from a distance, but slightly better defined when the walker is on the edge itself.

FOREST FAWR

Between the masses of Mynydd Ddu and the Brecon Beacons lies Forest Fawr, an upland plateau with several distinctive peaks, bounded by the A4067 to the west and the A470/A4059 to the east. There are some access problems to the peaks, for although the rounded hump of Fan Fawr can be ascended along clear paths, the way on to Fan Gyhirych, a far more impressive peak, is much less clear.

It is to the south that the area comes into its own. Here the limestone that once capped the entire area still remains. It is carboniferous limestone, the dissolvable, cave-producing rock, and produces the extraordinary spectacle, in the valleys of the Hepste and Mellte rivers, of whole rivers being swallowed. For many tens of metres at a stretch the rivers flow underground, the valley floor being dry with the occasional swallet hole allowing the visitor to hear and sometimes even glimpse the river. The limestone has occasionally been eaten away to reveal the underlying millstone grit. This harder rock, also occasionally exposed by geological faulting, produces waterfalls which serve to enhance the scenery still further. And as a last treat the country is low-lying so that the normal rich lime flora grows in abundance.

## Walk 18 Caves and Waterfalls

This magnificent walk, scenically one of the finest in the list, is straightforward, if a little arduous on occasions, and links together the best of the waterfalls on the Hepste and Mellte rivers, as well as visiting one of the most memorable cave entrances in Wales.

*Walk Category* : Intermediate (2 hours).

*Length* : 8 km (5 miles).

*Ascent* : 150 m  (500 ft).

*Maps* :  Landranger Sheet 160; Outdoor Leisure Sheet 11 Brecon
          Beacons Central Area.

*Starting and finishing point* :  The car-park at 929 125, reached by
turning left off the road that runs south from Ystradfellte, about 1 km ($^1/_2$
mile) south of the village. Ystradfellte itself is reached by a fine, but
narrow, road that links Heol Senni to Pontneddfechan and the A465
Heads of the Valleys road. The Heol Senni to Pontneddfechan road
passes between Fan Nedd and Fan Llia, two peaks of Forest Fawr, and
follows the Afon Llia, a major tributary of the Afon Hepste.

From the car-park a stile gives access to a steep, loose path to the River
Hellte and the cave entrance of Porth yr Ogof (see (1) Porth yr Ogof). The
cave entrance is easily reached by way of a conveniently located
rock shelf and is big enough to allow light to penetrate some way into
the cave, so that the intrepid boulder-hopper or the well-shod can get far
enough in to see the White Horse (see Note (1)), and to enjoy the view
back out through the entrance to the Mellte valley. **But please take note
of the warnings at the cave entrance, which are repeated in Note (1).**
    From the cave the walker must return to the car-park and then go back
to the road. Cross the road and take the obvious and well-worn path that
leads past several swallet holes (see (2) Swallet holes and clints and
grykes) to a rocky platform above the superb resurgence cave of the
Afon Mellte (see, also, Note (2)). Beyond the resurgence is a beautiful
section of limestone pavement (see, also, Note (2)). The pavement gives
way to a meadow where the river bank can be followed, crossing two
stiles to a footbridge. Do not cross the bridge, but continue along the
obvious track. To this point the walk has been through fine open country
with excellent flower-filled water meadows ringed by trees. Ahead now
is a superb section of deciduous wood, a fine setting for the waterfalls.
The first fall is soon reached, by taking the left-hand fork of a Y-junction
– the right fork appears to go the correct way, but is blind. This first fall
is Sgwd Clun-gwyn (see (3) The Clun-gwyn Falls).
    The path now crosses a couple of streams heading for the Afon Mellte

# WALK 18  CAVES AND WATERFALLS

YSTRADFELLTE

AFON MELLTE

N

PORTH YR OGOF ①

SWALLETS ②

⑤

S

S

RESURGENCE CAVE

S

S

S

FOOTBRIDGE

SGWD CLUN-GWYN ③

SGWD ISAF CLUN-GWYN ③

SGWD Y PANNWR ③

½    1Kr

½m

AFON HEPSTE

SGWD YR EIRA ③

SGWD ISAF CILHEPSTE ③

before reaching another Y-junction. The right-forking path reaches Sgwd Isaf Clun-gwyn (see, also, Note (3)), but it crosses steep ground, and there is no continuing path to the third falls so that the walker must retrace his route. Many will therefore take the left-hand fork and take a more long-range view of the second falls.

Beyond Sgwd Isaf Clun-gwyn the path rises steadily to reach a fenced forestry plantation. Soon a signed path going down and right off the main path visits the third falls (see (4) Sgwd y Pannwr), another out and back walk. The highlight of the walk now lies ahead. The path follows the forest edge around a distinct left corner. To the right here, and out of sight at the bottom of the wooded valley, the River Hepste is joining the Mellte, the abrupt corner being where the walk turns up the Hepste valley. Soon a steep, stepped path is reached to the right. Descend this with great care – it is loose and slippery, particularly after rain – to the Hepste river and a view of Sgwd yr Eira (see (5) Sgwd yr Eira). Many books tell the visitor that he can walk behind the falls and stay dry. In anything but the driest weather this story can be dismissed. To reach the falls a wet and tricky path must be followed underneath an overhanging cliff down which comes a soaking mini-falls, and the curtain of water on the left edge (as approached) of Sgwd yr Eira is more or less continuous. Once behind the falls however, the walker can stay fairly dry and admire one of the truly memorable experiences of walking in southern Wales. On the far side of the falls a path rises into wooded country. This can be followed for a reasonable view of yet another falls, Sgwd Isaf Cilhepste. This last falls is difficult to approach closely however, and the detour is only recommended to the particularly persistent falls-bagger.

### (1) *Porth yr Ogof*

Porth yr Ogof – the Door of the Cave – is the largest cave entrance in Wales, a slot of an entrance some 15 m (50 ft) wide and 5 m (16 ft) high. It is one of a large number of entrances to an extensive and still relatively unexplored cave system. The casual visitor can, with a little care, penetrate quite a long way inside the cave, certainly far enough to see the Pool of the White Horse. The pool is named because of the resemblance to a horse's head of a series of calcite streaks on its back wall. Legend has it that long ago a Welsh princess rode into the cave to escape a pursuer whose intentions towards her were a good deal less than honourable. Her horse stumbled and fell and both horse and rider were drowned. The horse's head was struck on the wall as a sad reminder.

The legend has one link with reality: the ease with which it is possible to drown in the cave. Experienced cavers with full equipment, including wet suits, and knowledge of cave-diving have died here because of the speed with which the system fills with water after heavy rain. The Mellte – the name, aptly, means lightning – is a curious river occasionally running underground along its length, and is prone to rapid rises in level if there is a storm on Forest Fawr. In times of flood the cave entrance can be almost filled with water and escape becomes impossible. **Please be careful** : a missed footing could be disastrous in the dark of the cave if the river is moving quickly and rising rapidly.

(2) *Swallet holes and clints and grykes*

The carboniferous limestone underlying the waterfall country is soluble in acids, and both the Mellte's water and rainwater are mildly acidic. Limestone is also a sedimentary rock, with a system of regular joints that offer a penetration path for the water. Over the course of millions of years the water eats away the rock, faster in some places than others because of variations in penetration rate, to form a variety of natural features. The most obvious are caves, and Porth yr Ogof (see Note (1) above) is the best example. Here an underground tunnel system has been carved out, the river disappearing from view for several hundred metres and returning to the surface in spectacular style at its cave resurgence.

Between the cave entrance and exit there are several swallet holes, where the dissolving process has been active vertically with a single joint being preferentially attacked to produce funnel-shaped holes. Such holes can lead to river-dissolved cave systems, and some of Britain's best pot-holes are entered by way of swallets. The name is a local Mendip one – and so preferred by the author! – but is only one of many given to the feature: swallow hole, pot-hole, sink hole, shake hole. Even on the Mendips it is a local name, being confined to the northern section: to the south of that area the holes are known as slockers (pronounced

'*slow-kerr*'). The underground river can occasionally be glimpsed, and most certainly heard, down the swallets, but do be cautious as the hole edges are unstable.

Where the attack on the limestone is less concentrated the weathering is more even, producing a limestone pavement where the joints have been more uniformly dissolved. Here steps of limestone, known as clints, are separated by deep slots, known as grykes. The best section of clints and grykes in Britain is that above Malham Cove in the Yorkshire Dales, but the section here is a good, if short, example.

### (3) *The Clun-gwyn Falls*

Sgwd Clun-gwyn, the Fall of the White Meadow, sometimes known as the Upper Clun-gwyn Falls, is an object lesson in waterfall formation. A geological fault has exposed a layer of soft shaley rock to the river whose bed here is no longer limestone but the less dissolvable sandstone. The shale has been eroded, the river now dropping 10 m (30 ft) in two leaps to reach the sandstone again. The fault, in addition to dropping the sandstone block by this distance, also inclined the beds so that the water flows towards the east bank. In wet weather this is barely noticeable, the river filling the shallow horseshoe, but in dry weather the fall is concentrated to the eastern side, to such an extent that it is possible to walk across the sandstone pavement at the fall edge.

Sgwd Isaf Clun-gwyn is the Lower Fall of the White Meadow and was formed over two parallel fault lines about 150 m apart. It is a spectacular fall, the river dropping nearly 30 m (90 ft) in two leaps, but changing direction as well, the fall line not being at right angles to the river. In addition, the river has eaten back into the pavements of the upper lip to form a tight gorge that prevents easy access to the fall, but increases its scenic appeal.

### (4) *Sgwd y Pannwr*

This is the Fuller's Fall, though quite why it should be so named is a mystery. It seems most unlikely that anyone would trek past two perfectly serviceable waterfalls to full his woollen cloth at this one. The most likely explanation is that the foaming base of the short fall reminded the locals of the foam that came off woollen cloth when it was

Sgwd Clun-gwyr

being washed after fulling.

### (5) *Sgwd yr Eira*

Sgwd yr Eira, the Fall of Snow, is a superstar waterfall and has attracted admiring descriptions over many years. I particularly like one from the early nineteenth century that speaks of the 'most remarkable natural object in Brecknockshire' with its 'noble cascade dashing in furious foam …throwing up clouds of spray and deafening the ear with its complaints'.

This fall too was produced by a geological fault, though here the exposed soft shale forms the back wall of the fall and has been eaten away by spraying and dripping water. This has exposed a hard rock platform along which the visitor can safely, if not exactly drily, walk. It is said that many years ago farmers herded their animals behind the falls in order to cross the Hepste. If true, then that would have been a most remarkable sight. From behind, the falls is extraordinary. Visits to famous places are often anti-climaxes, and this is, after all, only a curtain of water. Rest assured, at Sgwd yr Eira you will not be disappointed.


### BRECON BEACONS

The distinctive flat-topped peaks of the Brecon Beacons – that is the third mass of Old Red Sandstone which gives its name to the Park in which it lies – are the most recognisable feature of the Park. For many a mile along the Usk valley around Brecon town the peaks of Corn Du and Pen y Fan dominate the southern skyline. The mass is a reverse of that of Mynydd Ddu, the scarp slopes – and they are very steep indeed – being on the northern and western edges. What is different here is that the ice-sculpting of the scarps has produced a series of marvellous ridges. These ridges, such a feature of walks on the Beacons where they provide more satisfying approaches to the high peaks than on any of the other sandstone masses, enclose equally excellent cwms, their bottoms carved from V-shaped to U-shaped by the passage of ice. Surprisingly there is only one corrie lake, Llyn Cwm-llwch in the cwm formed by ridges running down from the two highest peaks.

To the east the scarp slope runs on much further than the casual visitor realises. The high peaks tend to attract like magnets, leaving a large area, almost half of the mass, largely unpopulated, even on good days. The views from this far end of the scarp are excellent, down into the Talybont valley, while the top itself, a narrow plateau produced by the scarp folding back on itself, is interesting for its weird peat deposits.

On the southern side, the Beacons' dip slope is steeper than on the other masses being, almost, a wide valley. This structure has been utilised by the water-gatherers, but offers equally good possibilities for the walker.

### Walk 19 Tommy Jones Memorial Walk

This walk is the 'trade route' up the two highest peaks of the Brecon Beacons and as such should be included in every visitor's itinerary. It also visits two memorials, profoundly different, but equally important in the statement they make. One is a memorial to a young child who died on the hill, the other records the gift of the hill to the people of Britain.

*Walk Category* : Intermediate/Difficult ($3^3/_4$ hours).

*Length* : $9^1/_2$ km (6 miles).

*Ascent* :  500 m (1600 ft).

*Maps* :  Landranger Sheet 160; Outdoor Leisure Sheet 11 Brecon Beacons Central Area.

*Starting and finishing point* : The car-park/picnic area beside the A470 Brecon to Merthyr Tydfil road. The car-park is at 988 199, to the east side of the road. There is another car-park near the Storey Arms Centre, at 983 203, a little way north.

In the car-park head south passing the toilet block to reach a track going left (east), about 50 m beyond the block, between the conifers. At the track end go through the kissing gate. To the left are the ruins of a World War II anti-aircraft position.

Y GRYN

600m  650m

600m

600m

LLYN
CWM-LLWCH

(19,3)

CO
(87

TOMMY
JONES MEMORIAL
(19,4)

700m

750m

800m

e

BWL
DUWY

550m

500m

450m

A470

STOREY
ARMS
(19,5)

S19

KG

NATIONAL TRUST
MEMORIAL
(19,1)

550m 600m 650m

700m

500m

450m

750m  800m

800m

750

½    1 Km

½m

Go half-right to reach a stream that is crossed by boulder-hopping. The crossing is distinctly less tricky if there has been a prolonged spell of dry weather. Beyond the stream the path is difficult to miss as it scars its way across peaty ground. The first memorial is reached (see (1) National Trust memorial), beyond which the track continues straightforwardly to Bwlch Duwynt, a col between Corn Du, to the left, and an unnamed peak to the right. In its earlier stages the ridge offers fine views to the gorge and shallow, shelved waterfalls of the Blaen Taf Fawr, while towards the top the long ridge of Craig Cwm-llwch holds the eye.

Go over Corn Du (see (2) Corn Du and Pen y Fan) and turn up to the trig point on top of Pen y Fan (see, also, Note (2)). Retrace your steps to Corn Du again, but here go right (north-west) to follow the beautiful sculpted ridge above Cwm-llwch (see (3) Cwm-llwch) along which the walker soon reaches the second memorial, (see (4) Tommy Jones memorial). Below the memorial a track leads off right, following the last of the Cwm-llwch ridge cliffs, but we take the leftward track that curves gently around the head of the shallow Blaen Taf Fawr cwm to reach a broad col below the shallow hump of Y Gyrn. There is a muddy stream crossing on the col, but the way is obvious, over Y Gyrn and down on a track that crosses two broken walls to reach a stile for the main A470. Go left, passing the Storey Arms (see (5) Storey Arms) to reach the start point car-park.

(1) *National Trust memorial*

As the plaque notes, the memorial commemorates the gift of 8150 acres of the Brecon Beacons to the National Trust by the Eagle Star Insurance Company. This gift, in 1965, has ensured continued access to these fine hills, and will be appreciated by all lovers of the countryside.

(2) *Corn Du and Pen y Fan*

Corn Du, the Black Horn, and Pen y Fan, the less elegantly named but marginally higher Hill of the Top, are formed of the Upper Series of Old Red Sandstone, from a particular type known as Plateau Bed. This is a (relatively) hard rock whose resistance has resulted in the distinctive 'table-top' structure of the peaks. On top of both peaks, and also on

The Tommy Jones memorial

nearby Cribyn, traces of Bronze Age cairns have been found dated to around 1800 BC. Little now remains visible to the casual visitor, though when excavated they revealed a number of urns containing the ashes of human cremations. It is thought that at the time of these Bronze Age folk the high summits of the Brecons could have supported farming. Today a cooler and wetter climate and gross overgrazing by sheep have reduced the land's productivity. From the summit of the peaks Cadair Idris and Plynlimon can be seen to the north, while southward Exmoor can be picked out across the Bristol Channel.

(3) *Cwm-llwch*

The steep, sculpted edges of Craig Cwm-llwch and Pen y Fan's north-western face make Cwm-llwch a superb example of a glacial cirque. Cirques are formed when originally existing hollows are gradually enlarged either by direct glacial action, or by being snow-filled with consequent frost-erosion. In the case of Cwm-llwch it certainly was glacially hollowed, the glacier-borne debris being deposited near the cwm outflow to form a morainic dam behind which Llyn Cwm-llwch formed when the last Ice Age ended.

(4) *Tommy Jones memorial*

On 4 August 1900 a Rhondda miner and his five-year-old son caught a train to Brecon to visit the miner's parents at their farm in Cwm-llwch. It was getting late as they began the 6 km (4 mile) walk to the farmhouse and by the time they reached Login, a now ruined house then in use as a soldiers' training camp, young Tommy Jones was tired. They rested and were met by Tommy's grandfather and his thirteen-year-old cousin Willie. Willie and Tommy set off alone to reach the farmhouse about $^1/_2$ km ($^1/_4$ mile) away, but as dusk fell Tommy was unnerved by the long shadows and started to cry. Willie had been told to alert the farm to the visitors' arrival, and so he let Tommy return to his father and grandfather alone. The boy had not arrived when Willie rejoined the older men about fifteen minutes later. Within twenty more minutes the Login soldiers were out searching. Next day the police and local folk joined in, but there was no sign of the boy. The search went on for weeks – Tommy's father did not go home for several weeks, and then

The path below Corn Du

returned each weekend – but without success. The *Daily Mail* offered a reward of £20 for news of Tommy and tales of kidnap and murder were rife. Finally, in September, a local woman dreamed about the boy, climbed the ridge of Craig Cwm-llwch, which she did not know, and discovered his remains. Tommy had climbed over 400 m (1300 ft), and walked at least 3 km (2 miles) to reach the remote spot where the memorial now stands. The obelisk was erected after a public collection. Mrs Hamer, the lady whose dream had led her to Tommy's body, gave money from the *Daily Mail* reward she had claimed, and the jury at Tommy's inquest all gave their fees.

The memorial is a simple, rough-hewn obelisk, a fine tribute. There are many walkers who are unable to pass it without a pause for thought. Tommy's five-year-old legs carried him a long way into very inhospitable country. It is difficult not to be moved by the thought of the boy, desperate to find his father, at first frightened, then panic-stricken as night fell, and finally exhausted. The hills occasionally exact a high price for their wild beauty.

(5) *Storey Arms*

Many years before the A470 brought visitors quickly from Brecon to Merthyr Tydfil, a green lane crossed the pass between the Beacons and Forest Fawr. This lane was used by drovers as well as those *en route* to market, and their thirsts were attended to in the Storey Arms, an inn named after a local family. Later, when the A470 was laid – as a turnpike road and not following the original green lane, the line of which can still be seen on the right bank of the Afon Tarell that drops down to join the Usk at Brecon – the inn became a café. Today it is an outdoor pursuits centre.

## Walk 20 The Neuadd Reservoirs

The long sculpted ridges on the northern face of the Brecon Beacons escarpment naturally attract most of the attention of visitors. The Brecons architecture is not straightforward however, the scarp edge being wrapped around at its eastern and western extremities, and the shallow dip slope being split by a valley that holds the two Neuadd reservoirs. Our route takes advantage of this unusual geography, following the scarp edge and visiting the highest tops, but staying on the dip slope throughout its length.

*Walk Category* : Difficult (5 hours).

*Length* : 16 km (10 miles).

*Ascent* :  750 mm (2450 ft).

*Maps* :  Landranger Sheet 160; Outdoor Leisure Sheet 11 Brecon Beacons Central  Area.

*Starting and finishing point* : The car-park beside the Blaen Taf Fechan river at 037 170. This is reached from Merthyr Tydfil along the western edge of the Pontsticill and Pentwyn reservoirs. At the northern tip of Pentwyn reservoir, as the road turns sharp right, a lane goes straight on. Follow this lane to the car-park. From the north the same turn is reached by taking a minor road from Talybont-on-Usk – on the B4558 Crickhowell to Brecon road – that goes along the edge of yet another reservoir.

From the car-park continue north-westerly towards the obvious mountain wall of the Brecons to reach the buildings at the tip of the Lower Neuadd reservoir. There is parking available here, but it is *ad hoc* and can cause access difficulties to the reservoir complex. Our route enters the reservoir compound by way of the gate, turning left to cross the reservoir outlet by footbridge to gain the grassy top of the dam itself. At the end of the dam a stile gives access to open country. Ahead now is a distinct, but thankfully not too eroded path, which heads off towards the corner of the forestry plantation on the left. At the plantation's top corner continue on to reach the ridge. Go right (north) and follow the edges of Craig Fan-ddu and Craig Gwaun Taf to reach the unnamed peak above Bwlch Duwynt. This scarp ridge walk is excellent, the cliffs of Craig Fan-ddu holding the interest until the ridge narrows down to an impressive sharpness, for sandstone country.

From Bwlch Duwynt the peaks Corn Du and Pen y Fan are reached easily (see Notes (2) and (3) of Walk 19). The trig point on top of Pen y Fan is set on a real table top, a table that is usually alive with people on good weekend days. To bear witness to the traffic the eastern ridge that we descend, along the top of the impressive cliffs of Craig Cwm Sere, is badly scarred (see (1) Path erosion).

From the col at the base of the ridge there is a straightforward and enjoyable walk up Cribyn. This is a fine peak, not quite high enough for a distinctive table top and so a more elegant shape. It is reached, from the north, by the superb ridge of Bryn Teg that is taken by Walk 21. Descend Cribyn's eastern ridge along the edge of Craig Cwm Cynwyn to reach a distinctive pass known as The Gap. If your day is a breezy one there will be a fair wind blowing through The Gap which you will turn into or away from as you turn right (south) onto a broad stony track (see (2) Roman road). The track follows along the length of the Neuadd reservoirs (see (3) Neuadd reservoirs) towards an obvious forestry plantation. Before this is reached a track goes off right for the *ad hoc* car-park near the reservoir gate. Ignore this, cross a broad stream gully – a bit of a scramble – to reach the plantation and continue along the track at its edge. This soon reaches the road. Go left to return to the car-park.

## (1) *Path erosion*

Path erosion is a problem in all of Britain's upland National Parks, a problem caused by the number of people who wish to enjoy the scenery of the Parks at first hand or, rather, foot! In the Beacons the problem is exacerbated by the nature of the underlying soil and rock. Unlike parts of North Wales where the rock is hard and the soil thin, here there is an appreciable topsoil though this is washed away as soon as the tramp of many feet has killed off the vegetation – a vegetation kept at minimal length by grazing. The action of washing away the soil causes ruts to form and widen and these become muddy and miserable. The walker, therefore, sadly but not unnaturally, takes to the ground on either side and the process begins again.

Erosion is a problem with no easy solution. If the Park Authorities attempt to stabilise the soil by any of a number of means the artificiality

The Brecon Beacons from the north-east

of the techniques is often decried. Yet the only other solution would be an access ban that lasted many years, perhaps even decades; and hard-won access to the hills is unlikely to be relinquished without a contest. Perhaps it is best to recognise that erosion-stabilising programmes are necessary and to be helpful and tolerant of them, and to keep rigidly to the paths and suggested detours.

(2) *Roman road*

There is an old tradition that the track that takes The Gap to breach the mountain wall of the Beacons follows a Roman road. It is certainly true that the Romans had a presence in the area, and that one way of reaching the fort of Cicutium, at 003 297 near Y Gaer about 4 km ($2^1/_2$ miles) west of Brecon, would have been to go through The Gap, especially if the intention was to find the most direct way to another fort near Merthyr Tydfil. There is, however, no evidence to support the claim.

(3) *Neuadd reservoirs*

The lower reservoir, the smaller and closer to the start point, was completed in 1884 to supply water to Merthyr Tydfil, then a boom town of the coal and steel industries. As the industrial expansion continued a second reservoir was required and the upper dam was constructed. The upper reservoir was then, and is now, but only occasionally, known as 'Zulu' for no better reason, apparently, than that its construction coincided with the Zulu Wars!

## Walk 21 Bryn Teg

Walks 19 and 20 explore the best routes to the high peaks of the Brecon Beacons, while Walk 22 below explores the high land at the range's eastern end. That would seem to be enough, but there is one more walk on the Beacons, included for no better reason than that it climbs the best ridge and descends above the best cwm.

*Walk category* : Difficult ($4^1/_2$ hours).

*Length* : 14 km (9 miles).

*Ascent* : 650 m (2130 ft).

*Maps* :  Landranger Sheet 160; Outdoor Leisure Sheet 11, Brecon
            Beacons Central Area.

*Starting and finishing point* : Cantref church, at  056 255 on the road
from Llanfrynach that runs west to join the A470 near Libanus. Parking
is limited and not easy; please be careful. Aternatives are to use the area
at the end of the road beyond Bailea, at 038 237 and at the end of the
road beyond Llwyn Fren, at 058 241.

From the church (see (1) Cantref church) go east, back towards
Llanfrynach, taking a track to the right after about 50 m. Follow the
track to a footbridge over the Afon Cynrig and go diagonally across the
field beyond to a stile. Go left and follow the track to a lane. Go right on
the lane following it past Llwynycelyn Farm to a Y-junction. Either fork
can be taken, the right fork over a stream leading to a very sharp left turn
or a lane through Neuadd Farm, past Bailea to the road end. The left
turn reaches Tir-ciw (Cantref Gallery) where the metalled lane ends.
From here a green lane, difficult in places, leads to a gate and the road
end near the entrance to Cwncynwyn farm. A stony track now leads
south to reach a gate for open country. Ahead now is Bryn Teg, one of
the most beautiful ridges in Wales. The translation of the name is
Beautiful Hill, so I am not the first to hold this opinion.
  Follow Bryn Teg to Cribyn's summit and then go left (east) to The
Gap, following Walk 20. At The Gap continue eastward, climbing up
towards Craig Cwm-oergwm to reach the top of the Cefn Cyff ridge, a
point known as Fan y Big, a fine viewpoint. Descend Cefn Cyff, with the
magnificent Cwm Oergwm to the right. The ridge descends steeply,
flattens out and then falls steeply again. On this last section keep a line
of trees to the right and head for a soon obvious gate. Go through this
and down the stony track beyond. Soon another gate is reached, beyond
which is a metalled lane. Go left on this and follow it for 1200 m ($^3/_4$
mile) to where a lane goes off left. Take this and after about 250 m, as
the lane bends left, take the track to the right. This is the outward route
which is retraced to the church.

# WALK 21   BRYN TEG

(1) *Cantref church*

The Church of St Mary, Cantref, beautifully set with an approach path through an avenue of fine yew trees, has an early seventeenth century tower, but much of the rest is new, the nave having been rebuilt and much altered in the nineteenth century by Charles Buckeridge who was responsible for the renovation of several other churches in the area. Inside there is an interesting font, perhaps from as early as the twelfth century, though with some overlaying work that suggests that it was reworked at a later time. The churchyard has a number of interesting table tombs and is reached through a delightful, if curious wrought-iron gate.

## Walk 22 The Eastern Beacons

Not surprisingly the high tops of the Beacons, Corn Du and Pen y Fan, attract the majority of visitors. This, together with the fact that The Gap seems to offer a logical eastern end point of the range, means that the huge plateau to the east of The Gap is more rarely visited. In fact this plateau offers fine walking with a distinctly different, almost lunar landscape.

*Walk Category* : Difficult ($4^1/_2$ hours).

*Length* : 12 km ($7^1/_2$ miles).

*Ascent* :  550 m (1800 feet).

*Maps* :  Landranger Sheet 160; Outdoor Leisure Sheet 11 Brecon
                  Beacons Central Area.

*Starting and finishing point* : Either of the two car-parks at 064 170 or 056 175 on the minor road from Talybont-on-Usk that is also used to reach the start of Walk 20. The walk actually goes through both car-parks – it could, in principle, be shortened by a few hundred metres if the second-metalled car-park is used – but in the author's opinion the first car-park gives the more satisfactory start.

From the car-park go back to the road and go right and down towards Pont Blaen-y-glyn. Just before the bridge a stile, left, gives access to a path that follows the Caerfanell stream back uphill. A slab bridge crosses the Nant Bwrefwr just before it reaches the Caerfanell, and beyond it there is a Y-junction of paths. That to the right visits the noisy waterfall (see (1) Waterfalls), but is taken by our return route. Take the left-hand path, therefore, which is marked with painted posts, to reach the road into the second car-park. Go right along the road, but before reaching the car-park take a track left that runs between the Nant Bwrefwr and the forestry plantation. Along this track there are good views of more waterfalls (see, also, Note (1) Waterfalls).

As the forestry plantation ends the path bears rightward (north) away from the Nant Bwrefwr and up the broad ridge of Craig y Fan Ddu. The views from the ridge, especially to the east and back down the route, are exhilarating, and there are fine local views when the broken cliffs to the right edge closer in on the path. This cliff edge is now followed – there is a boggy section where a plateau-draining stream crosses the path for the plateau  edge – to Bwlch y Ddwyallt. There is a bewildering array of paths here, but none is needed for the moment as we cross to the northern scarp slope for a marvellous view out across the double cwms of Oergwm and Cwareli.

To the right (east) now is a magnificent peat plateau (see (2) Peat hags), bounded on all sides by steep, broken cliffs. There is a trig point on top of an unnamed peak at 066 202 and another peak, more poorly defined but one whole metre higher, at 062 209. At 062 200 is a memorial as poignant in its way as that to Tommy Jones that we passed on Walk 19 (see (3) War memorial). From there, or from any other point on the plateau, the walker must reach the well-defined point at 066 192 where the cliffs of Cwar y Gigfran and Gwalciau'r Cwm meet. From there a groove – probably the remains of a 'slipway' from the time when sandstone was quarried from the cliffs near the spur – leads down and right. Follow the groove to a fence and follow that to a stile. Go over and follow the stream down to a footbridge. Go over the bridge and the stile beyond to reach a path that is followed back past the fine, noisy waterfall

Bryn Teg and Cribyn

(see (1) Waterfalls) mentioned in our outward journey. Beyond the fall the path reaches the outward path. Go left to return to the car-park.

## (1) *Waterfalls*

The largest waterfall, with a drop of 15 m (50 ft) in total, is a narrow fall, the water landing on an impressive pavement of rock, a by-product of local glaciation. The Nant Bwrefwr's waterfalls are smaller but equally fine. The first, which is split up by numerous jagged columns of rock, is especially good, supporting a fine collection of mosses and other damp-loving plants.

## (2) *Peat hags*

Peat is produced where plant material has been broken down by the processes of decay in a wet environment. In the absence of sufficient oxygen the normal bacteria and fungi that accelerate decay are absent or limited and instead of rotting away the dead plant material 'humifies' to a jelly-like mass. If this jelly is now pressurised by overlying rocks coal is formed. If there is no overlying material to produce large pressures the jelly instead forms large compact bogs. If the peat is then cut it dries to a stringy dark-brown cake that is useful as a fuel or to the gardener. Here on the eastern Beacons after the production of a peat bog perhaps 6000 years ago the climate became drier, and local drainage was aided by the early farmers. The peat has therefore dried naturally. In this state it is very easily weathered and ice, frost, wind and rain have created large ruts in the bog. There is no evidence of peat cutting here, so the weathering we see is completely natural. Some of the weathered hags are remarkable: as high as a short walker and weirdly shaped, a bit like surreal mushrooms. As a piece of extraordinary natural architecture it is worth coming many a mile to see.

## (3) *War memorial*

The mountains of Wales were a favoured area in World War II for the training of air crews in low-level flying, and as an area where resting crews could keep their hand in. Sadly the Welsh weather took its toll of these crews and several mountains have the remains of planes that came to grief. Perhaps the best-known memorial is that on the summit of Arenig Fawr further to the north, because this memorial on the Beacons is off the beaten track. It is to Wellington bomber R1465, a survivor of

German raids with 214 Squadron which crashed here in low cloud during a night-time training exercise. The bits of twisted metal are a last reminder of the plane: the crew were all killed, their bodies being moved from the plateau for burial.

## THE LLANGATTOCK ESCARPMENT

Immediately east of the Brecon Beacons, indeed connected to it, the walker being able to walk, road-free, from one to the other, is another section of the limestone sheet that once covered the Old Red Sandstones. On the scarp slope above Llangattock the limestone has been quarried and from the Usk valley near Crickhowell the view south is dominated by a line of low, vertical cliffs that contour around the hill just below the skyline. The limestone is carboniferous, and the quarrymen broke into numerous caves which have been explored to yield one of Britain's most significant caving areas. On top of the quarried cliffs there are frequent pools in the plateau. It is an odd discovery, indeed totally unexpected: how can water lie in small pools when only yards away it has dissolved its way into the rock to form extensive caves? The answer is straightforward. Just south of the cliffs the limestone sheet has itself been overlain with a sheet of impervious Millstone Grit. This harder, less easily weathered rock forms a poor soil and the area of Mynydd Llangattock and Mynydd Llangynidr is boggy country with little vegetation apart from stiff ling. It is a wild, vaguely hostile country, offering fine uncompromising walking.

## Walk 23 Chartists' Cave

The plateau-like land beyond the escarpment that sits above the Usk valley is split into two halves by a road across it from Beaufort, near Brynmawr, to Llangynidr. Each half offers a fine, if rugged, walk on rarely visited moorland. Our first walk takes the western half, visiting a cave that could have had historical significance. This walk is not for the

The high Beacons from the eastern plateau

inexperienced if the weather is poor. Good visibility is required unless it is to be followed solely by use of a compass – a procedure which rather defeats the object, even if it is good practice – and it is better not to tackle the walk after continuous heavy rain which can make the going arduous and very wet.

*Walk category* : Intermediate/Difficult (3 hours).

*Length* : 11 km (7 miles).

*Ascent* : 250 metres (800 feet).

*Maps* : Landranger Sheet 161; Outdoor Leisure Sheets 11 and 13 Breco Beacons Central and Eastern Areas.

*Starting and finishing point* : At 160 164 on the minor road from Beaufort, near Brynmawr, to Llangynidr, on the B4558 Crickhowell to Brecon 'back road'. This plateau-crossing minor road is unfenced and studded with parking spaces. That suggested is close to the quarry at 159 163 which is the first objective of the walk.

Take the track to the old stone quarry – care is needed in the quarry itse as there is an unprotected pot-hole in its floor – and climb out of its bac by going to the left of the cave. From the top an indistinct track leads of southward – on a bearing of 205°– passing a spectacular series of swalle or shake holes (see Note (2) of Walk 18) many 15–20 m (50–60 ft) deer **Please be careful**, the holes are not all well protected and their edges can be unstable.

From the top of the small rise ahead the Llangynidr reservoir can be seen – if the weather is clear  – and this gives the line. The reservoir is fenced, so follow the fence westward towards the reservoir tip where an inflowing stream is crossed.  Westward now, on a bearing of 275°, ther is a large pile of stones on the skyline. Head for this and continue past i on the same bearing, heading for the small lake of Llyn y Garn-fawr at 126 149. In dry weather – when the walk is at its easiest – this lake can dry up completely, but there is a large pile of stones at its southern end

which gives the line in clear weather.

From the lake's northern tip Chartists' Cave is a mere 300 m away on a bearing of 30°, but do not be deceived, the cave can be very difficult to find. From the cave (see (1) Chartists' Cave) the return journey is more straightforward – on a clear day. On a bearing of 75° the trig point at 147 159 is visible and is the next objective. There are indistinct tracks in this area, but nothing is really better than a direct route across the moor. From the trig point the quarry is on a bearing of 77°, though things become easier the closer the walker is to it.

## (1) *Chartists' Cave*

The Poor Law of 1834 caused great resentment among poor working people throughout Britain because its implication was not only that the poor were responsible for their poverty but that they should be made to suffer for it. The resentment was seen in the growth of unionism, and also in the birth of Chartism. Chartists were those who supported the People's Charter of 1838, a six-point charter calling for full male suffrage, secret ballots, and the abolition of property qualifications for Members of Parliament. Today the requests seem reasonable enough but the threat they posed to the established order in 1838 was enormous. The local Chartists' leader in South Wales was John Frost, a strong-willed man of fifty-five. In late 1839 Frost was convinced that Chartists all over the country were about to rise up and seize power and so he organised an armed uprising to take Newport, then the region's largest town. Legend has it that Frost and the other leaders stayed in the cave here during the last days before the march, and that other caves in the Llangattock escarpment held men making weapons. Frost had hoped that 50,000 men would follow him to Newport, but in the event on a cold and miserably wet November day there were a great deal fewer. How many exactly is open to conjecture. Frost maintained there were only 400, though the Mayor of Newport claimed that there were 20,000. As each side had a vested interest in exaggeration it is likely that the real figure was about 5,000, most of them armed, if at all, only with pitchforks.

The Chartists marched to the Westgate Hotel and were met there by the Mayor and a squad of soldiers. Words were exchanged and then a shot was fired. Later each side blamed the other for the shot but that is academic now. The soldiers opened fire killing around twenty of the men. Frost was arrested – the 'rebellion' was over. At his trial Frost, together with several others, was sentenced to death, but recognition that this would create martyrs meant that the sentences were commuted to transportation for life to Tasmania. In fact Frost served fifteen years, returning to Britain to live to the ripe old age of ninety-three and remaining strong-willed to the last.

Whether the cave was actually used by the Chartists' leaders or not, it is an interesting site. The numerous markers that frequently adorn its entrance attest to its use by orienteers, while cavers occasionally visit it to explore its 120 m (400 ft) of passageway.

## Walk 24 The Llangattock Quarries

This walk takes the eastern half of the high plateau above the Usk Valley. In its early stages it is well defined, following an old tramway past some good industrial relics, a unique nature reserve and the entrances to some fine caves. Thereafter it ascends the plateau to visit a mysterious lake. As with the last walk the plateau is no place to be if the weather is poor, the more so in this case as the cliffs of the old quarries start abruptly and are both vertical and high.

*Walk Category* : Intermediate/Difficult ($2^1/_2$ hours).

*Length* : 10 km (6 miles).

*Ascent* : 200 m (650 ft).

*Maps* : Landranger Sheet 161; Outdoor Leisure Sheet 13 Brecon Beacons Eastern Area.

*Starting and finishing point* : From Brynmawr a mountain road runs around the Llangattock escarpment before dropping down into Llangattock village and continuing to Crickhowell. The road is a fine outing in itself: at the Brynmawr end there are magnificent views out over the Usk Valley and the Black Mountains, while the drop is a first-

class test of driving skills, being both steep and narrow – and
occasionally both together – and having unyielding walls on both sides.
If you meet someone coming the other way it can be great fun. On this
road, at 209 155 there is an obvious stony track going up towards the
quarries. Park at any convenient place near the bottom of this. There are
more places on the Brynmawr side (the eastern side) of the incline.
Please park tidily.

From your parking place return to the bottom of the track and take it to a
ruined building near its top. This is the ruin of an old limekiln and dates
from the time when the quarries were in full production (see (1)
Llangattock Quarries). Behind the ruin is the Darren Quarry, but we do
not visit it, going, instead, to the right on a rough track, sometimes
grassy, sometimes stony, along which once ran a quarry tramway. To the
left, just after leaving the building, there is a break in the otherwise
continuous quarry wall. The return route uses this break to drop through
the cliffs.
   The old tramway veers off to the Pant-y-Rhiw Quarry and although it
is possible to take a direct line, to the right of the now grassy spoil
cones, it is worth visiting the quarry itself. It is popular with outdoor
centres and there are frequently hordes of trainee rock climbers at work
on its walls. At the left (east) end is a small pond that is favoured by
dragonflies, while at its right (west) end the line of cliffs is almost
breached by the debris of a massive rock fall that occurred in the late
'40s. Near this landslip, and more especially in the continuation of the
quarry beyond, there are superb flowstone formations on the upper
quarry walls.
   Beyond the formidable wall of the continuation quarry, the cliff wall is
more broken. This is Craig y Cilau, a National Nature Reserve (see (2)
Craig y Cilau). Beneath the cliffs here the old tramway appears again,
offering a straightforward way of reaching, at 193 154, the huge entrance
of Eglwys Faen, one of the numerous caves that are found in the
escarpment (see (3) Quarry caves). Another cave entrance, to Agen
Allwedd (see, also, Note (3)), is reached at 187 158. In contrast to the
easily accessible Eglwys Faen, the entrance here is gated to prevent
inexperienced explorers from gaining access to one of Britain's longest

cave systems. Beyond Agen Allwedd the tramway ends, though progress is still possible along the cliff base. To gain the top of the cliffs it is necessary to continue to the clear cliff left-turn at 183 167 and then for another 500 m to where the fading cliffs give way to steep, but easily climbed, slopes. An alternative to this extension is to take an obvious, but exposed, route up the steep track just beyond Agen Allwedd. This track is clear enough but can be dangerous if wet or icy. If using it, please take great care.

Whether the long route or the steep track is taken, the walker should walk back (eastward) along the cliff edge until a steep gully blocking progress is reached. Now head south-west – along the line of the gully – to reach a small pool, often dry in summer, and the impressive swallet or shake hole of Waen Rudd (see Note (2) of Walk 18). Those used to the swallets of Walk 23 will be stunned by the sheer size of Waen Rudd. Water that sinks here reappears in the entrance series of Agen Allwedd.

From Waen Rudd go due south across the moor to reach Pwll Gwy-rhoc, a brown lake that seems to lurk among the heather. Though I have used the now prevalent spelling I am inclined to believe that it is a fanciful rendering of *gwrhoc* , Welsh for witch, and that seems entirely appropriate for this vaguely mysterious body of water. Even its existence, within a few hundred metres of one of the most extensive caving areas in Britain, an area where the rock is readily dissolvable, seems odd. In reality the pool lies on a bed of impermeable Millstone Grit that overlies the carboniferous limestone southward from here.

From the pool, head south-east to the obvious high ground and follow a shallow ridge to the trig point summit of Mynydd Pen-cyrn. The ridge has one or two Bronze Age cairns on it and the distinctly more recent scars from the laying of an underground gas pipe. From the summit go east to reach an indistinct track that heads northward to reach the safe descent through the line of quarry cliffs that we noted on the outward route. Follow the outward route back to the start.

Craig y Cilau

## (1) *Llangattock Quarries*

The taking of stone from the Llangattock escarpment probably began in earliest times, the stone being readily available as the steep slope produced rock outcrops. It was not until the early nineteenth century, however, that the commercial exploitation of the escarpment started. The opening of the Brecon and Abergavenny Canal – followed by Walk 31 – gave quarrymen easy access to markets, and a tramway was built from the quarries to Llangattock Wharf. In all, three inclines were built, each powered by gravity, i.e. full trolleys going down to the wharf pulled a number of empty trolleys up the incline.

It was not stone that was the chief export, but lime, used for 'sweetening' agricultural land. Most of the lime was produced by burning the stone at the wharf, a fairly logical procedure as coal could be unloaded from canal barges directly into the kilns. Later however a kiln was constructed at the Darren Quarry. Presumably it was calculated that hauling coal up the incline was worth the effort, the downward-travelling trolleys being able to carry far more finished lime than raw stone.

By the 1830s the need for lime for agriculture had become secondary, the growth of the iron industry in South Wales now requiring vast quantities of limestone as a furnace flux. The quarries at Llangattock were extended, new tramways were built and the area became very prosperous. The boom was relatively short-lived: within fifty years more efficient ways of making steel reduced the need for limestone. The need for agricultural lime kept the quarries active at a reduced level, but by the early years of this century even that requirement was decreasing. In 1920 the last shipment of stone was burnt at Llangattock Wharf and, soon after, the quarries were silent.

Today the escarpment is a fascinating place for the industrial archaeologist. There are old buildings, old inclines and tramways –now mainly grassed over, but their tracks still visible – spoil heaps and even the odd rarity: just below the tramway as it nears Pant-y-Rhiw Quarry a rusting pair of lines disappear into a tight horizontal mine shaft. But the site is also a dangerous one and extreme caution should be exercised by anyone intending to explore the buildings, caves and shafts.

(2) *Craig y Cilau*

The English translation of the Welsh is Refuge Crag which is entirely apt, if fortuitous. The cliffs here are steep enough to prevent sheep grazing, but not vertical, so that a quite remarkable plant culture has survived. Alpine enchanter's nightshade is at its British southern limit on the cliffs and here too are angular Solomon's Seal, thistle broomrape and maiden pink. The chief delight are the trees. There is a small beech wood – one of Europe's most westerly stands – lime, both large- and small-leaved, and yew. There are also six species of *sorbus* , the fairly common rowan (mountain ash) and five rare varieties. Two of these are known only in Powys, while one, *Sorbus minima* , is virtually confined to this area. The tree, a lesser whitebeam, was 'discovered' in the late nineteenth century by the Revd Augustine Ley and was believed to have become extinct when a large rock-fall destroyed all known specimens about forty years ago. Thankfully a few specimens did survive, and there are now several trees on the cliff.

In 1959 the special nature of Craig y Cilau was recognised when the site – a total of 157 acres – was made a National Nature Reserve. There is unrestricted access for the public, but it goes without saying that every care should be taken to avoid damage not only to the trees, shrubs and plants, but to the cliffs themselves. The collecting of plants is forbidden without permission of the Nature Conservancy.

3) *Quarry caves*

The limestone of the Llangattock escarpment is carboniferous, the form that dissolves readily in acidic water. Not surprisingly then there are caves here, many of which have been broken into by the quarrying operations. What is surprising is that the cave systems are so extensive that Llangattock is now one of the most important caving centres in Britain. Ogof-y-Darren Cilau, at 206 153 behind the ruined limekiln at the start of the walk, starts with a long, tight, wet crawl of the type that makes cavers purr with delight and gives non-cavers the heebie-jeebies at the very thought. The cave is now explored for over 6 km (4 miles). Eglwys Faen – the Stone Church – which our walk passes is, by contrast, only about 1 km (1100 yards) long. The huge entrance beside the tramway is one of several into the cave and leads directly to a vast chamber that presumably gives the cave its name. The casual visitor can penetrate some distance into the chamber guided by light streaming in through the entrance, but do take care: the ground is uneven and boulder-strewn. Elsewhere the cave has an aven, an upper passage, reached by one member of the party ascending a vertical squeeze in order to let down a ladder through a hole in the roof for other members to climb.

Agen Allwedd, whose gated entrance we also pass, is the largest local system at 25 km (15 miles). At one time Aggie, as it is known in caving circles, was the longest cave in Britain, but it has long since lost that title to Ogof Ffynnon Ddu, the cave near the start of Walk 15. The cave's name means Keyhole Cleft, a reference to its original entrance that was shaped like a keyhole. The cave reputedly contains a chamber large enough to house St Paul's Cathedral, reached by a passage so tight that it can only be negotiated with perseverance and difficulty.

THE BLACK MOUNTAINS

The last, the easternmost block of Old Red Sandstone is a fine large mass with a northern scarp slope as elsewhere, and a long shallow dip slope ending more steeply into the Usk valley. Here however the Sandstone block has been river-carved and a series of essentially north-south valleys has been formed. The effect of this has been to produce a hand-like structure with a series of finger ridges pointing south joined across the northern scarp edge. To the east is one ridge of the Vale of Ewyas, the ridge taken by the Offa's Dyke long-distance footpath and terminating at Hay Bluff. The Vale of Ewyas carries a road that crosses the northern scarp, by way of Gospel Pass, its western side being formed by a ridge that divides Ewyas from the Grwyne Fawr valley. Next are two ridges joined at Waun Fach, the highest summit on the mass, that define the valley of the Grwyne Fechan that flows past Llanbedr. West of the ridge from Waun Fach to Pen Cerrig-calch is the valley of the Rhian-goll taken by the A479. This valley's western side is defined by the Black Mountains' most westerly ridge.

The well-defined and low-lying valleys give the Black Mountains a gentle pastoral feel. By contrast the defining ridges give long upland walks, though they do offer excellent conditions under foot.

## Walk 25 Mynydd Troed

Those who have travelled on the A479 from Talgarth to Crickhowell will know that as they twist and turn upwards out of Talgarth they have before them one of the most perfect ridges in Wales, an apparent knife edge to a conical peak. Things are not as they seem, as we shall see, but the ridge of Mynydd Troed does offer a superb walk, and is short enough to use as a gentle introduction to the hill-walking of the Brecon Beacons National Park.

*Walk Category* : Easy ($2^1/_2$ hours).

*Length* : 8 km (5 miles), though shorter if the full ridge is not walked.

*Ascent* : 350 m (1150 ft).

*Maps* :  Landranger Sheet 161; Outdoor Leisure Sheet 13 Brecon Beacons Eastern Area.

*Starting and finishing point* : Almost at the top of the pass that the A479 from Talgarth to Crickhowell takes to cross the Black Mountains there is a telephone box on the east side. Beside this is a lay-by with parking for several cars.

From the lay-by go south, i.e. towards Crickhowell, and take the first lane on the right- hand (west) side, after about 150 m. Follow this, going through a gated compound, to open country. Here the path goes ahead — we take it on our return journey – but we go left to tackle the ridge of Mynydd Troed. Sadly the ridge turns out to be much broader than it looks and leads to a summit that is, in fact, only the high end point of a long north-south running ridge. Nevertheless the walk is a fine one and the summit is a fine vantage point (see (1) Mynydd Troed). To get full benefit from the peak's position it is best to walk south along the ridge. A full-length walk – to the point at which the gently sloping ridge falls much more steeply – involves a round trip of about 3 km (2 miles) and an ascent of 60 m (200 ft) on the return leg. The walk can therefore be

# WALK 25    MYNYDD TROED

G G

Ⓢ

← T

350m

400m

450m
500m
550m
600m

Ⓐ

MYNYDD
TROED ①
(609m)

550m

½        1 Km

½ m

shortened by that amount if the ridge is not traversed.

To descend go south of the trig point to reach a path that descends the west flank of the hill to reach the path that we left on the outward journey. Go right and follow it back to the start.

### (1) *Mynydd Troed*

The importance of the uplands of Wales to the Celts is detected in the number of words they had to describe meadows and hills, each one unique in its description of the countryside and its usefulness for agriculture or defence. For hills there are *pen, twyn, carnedd* and *moch* – to name only the major ones – each with a fairly indifferent translation into English. The peak here is a *mynydd*, usually translated as a mountain, which is a rather grand title for an elongated grassy ridge that just fails to reach the 2000 ft contour. *Troed* means leg or foot and could (just) refer to the shapely elegance of the ridge when seen from the Talgarth side.

From the peak the view of the Rhian-goll valley and the far wall of the Black Mountains is superb, perhaps the best from any vantage point on the range – though that on Walk 29 is also a front runner – while the view northward over the Wye valley and the Welsh Marches is equally good. Eastward the position of the peak, at the western extremity of the range, means that there are extensive views over pleasant farmland. Llyn Syfaddan, or Llangorse Lake as it is more usually known, is also visible. This is the largest natural lake in South Wales and a place of legend. One local tale is of a village that stood where the lake now is, but was swallowed by an earthquake and now rests below the water. When the water is rough the old church bell can be heard chiming and an old woman from the village occasionally surfaces to kidnap a child. The latter part of the tale of the Old Woman of the Lake has, apparently, been used to frighten the local kids with a slight change to her behaviour, so that she only kidnaps disobedient children! Interestingly it is now known that there was once a village on the *crannog,* a man-made island, that lies close to the lake's northern shore. It was almost certainly a Celtic village and the dating of a dug-out canoe found at the site suggests that it could have been inhabited as late as AD 800. Could it be that a folk memory of a village on the *crannog* gave rise to the legend of the submerged village?

Gerald of Wales mentioned the lake and as a good lover of legends noted that it occasionally turned bright green and was also occasionally streaked with blood-red. In winter, he said, it moo-ed like a herd of cows. It is probable that each of these stories has a basis in truth, the colour changes being algal 'blooms', the noise being ice cracking. More likely to be a real legend is his story that the birds of the lake will sing only for the rightful king of Wales.

As a natural lake Llangorse – which Gerald called Brecknock Mere or Clamosus – has a superb collection of water plants, fish and birds. The fish were famous for their immense size, the local expression for conveying hugeness being *cyhyd a llyswen syfaddan,* as long as a Syfaddan eel. Sadly 'has' is almost becoming 'had', as the lake has no protection as a national site and is a centre for all sorts of water sports which interfere with the birds and destroy the vegetation. With so many artificial sheets of water in South Wales it is a shame that Llangorse could not have been left alone.

## Walk 26 Waun Fach

The elongated ridges of the Black Mountains make circular walks difficult, and horseshoe walks – taking the line of the northern scarp slope to link ridges – long. The very best walk is to start at Llanbedr (see Walk 27) and to take the Crug Mawr ridge to Waun Fach, returning over Table Mountain. That is a very long trip and outside the scope of this book. Instead we shall explore that same country in two walks. That has the distinct advantage, the ascent of one of the most delightful ridges in South Wales.

On the A479 from Talgarth to Crickhowell it is the sharp ridge of Mynydd Troed (Walk 25) that takes the eye. If instead the traveller is going north, from Crickhowell to Talgarth, the eye is drawn to a peaked ridge that leads west-east as a buttress to the long north-south Black Mountains ridge. Our walk takes that ridge, and visits the highest peaks of the Black Mountains range.

Mynydd Troed

*Walk Category* : Difficult (5 hours).

*Length* : 16 km (10 miles).

*Ascent* :  750 m  (2450 ft).

*Maps* :  Landranger Sheet 161; Outdoor Leisure Sheet 13 Brecon
         Beacons Eastern Area.

*Starting and finishing point* : At the telephone box, as for Walk 25.

From the telephone box walk south, but here take the first lane leftward
(east). Bear left at the lane junction and continue to the entrance to Dinas
Farm. Do not go in, but follow the lane around the farm on its right
(east) side and up to a gate. Beyond the gate is open land. Go up the
obvious ridge ahead, the start of the 'skyline ridge' of Y Grib. The first
ridge has a distinct false summit and a descent to Bwlch Bach-a'r-Grib
from which there is a magnificent gentle ridge walk all the way to Pen y
Manllwyn.

   Pen y Manllwyn is not a real peak, just the last hump on a broad ridge
that falls northward from Waun Fach. Go right (south-east) and follow
the ridge to the summit of Waun Fach (see (1) Waun Fach and Pen y
Gadair Fawr). From the summit, more a broad plateau than a top, the
huge cairn on top of Pen y Gadair Fawr is visible to the south-east. To
reach it and return means an out-and-back walk, but who could resist
such a summit?

   From Pen y Gadair Fawr (see, also, Note (1)) return to Waun Fach and
from the summit go just west of north to reach the newly emerged
stream of Rhian-goll which is followed downhill. Below the third rock
outcrop (at 201 304) go off left, following an indistinct track that reaches
a gate in the common fence at 195 301. Go through the gate and follow
the lane beyond. The lane swings left to reach a farmhouse, just before
which go right to cross a bridge over the Rhian-goll. Just beyond the
bridge leave the lane by going left along a track that is usually churned
up by the hooves of the numerous ponies from the local pony-trekking
centres. Along the lane watch for a stile on the left side that gives access

to Castell Dinas (see (2) Castell Dinas). There is no right of way to the site, the stile and path constituting a permissive path of the landowner. This is a very generous act by the landowner and one which all walkers will appreciate. It is imperative that everyone visiting the site should remember the responsibility that his presence places upon him. It is on his actions that the next walker may be judged.

From Castell Dinas return to the lane and follow it to the common gate used on the outward journey. Go left and follow the outward journey back to the start.

### (1) *Waun Fach and Pen y Gadair Fawr*

The summit of Waun Fach, the Little Moor, cannot readily be called the high spot of the Black Mountains, even if it is the highest spot. The actual top is marked by a thick, circular trig point base set among a morass of churned-up peat. The slab usually has daubs of colour, presumably for the pony-trekkers who pass this way regularly in small herds. Though the hooves of the ponies are responsible for the churning it is not wholly their fault: long before pony-trekking was popular Waun Fach could be a muddy place, the thin soil being easily eroded to reveal the peaty moorland of the name.

Pen y Gadair Fawr suffers less from unnatural erosion and is, in any case, a more sharply defined and therefore better drained peak. Its summit cairn is a wonder of the cairn builder's art and is a good place to take in the view. To the east the valley of the Grwyne Fechan is heavily afforested – though the visitor to it will find it a delightful mix of hard and soft woods at stream level – and finishes with a small reservoir. The Llanbedr valley to the west is more pastoral. From Waun Fach the distinctive cone of Sugar Loaf can be seen, and there is a fine view along the continuous scarp line to the north.

### (2) *Castell Dinas*

The Castell Dinas hill fort stands on a final detached knob of the Y Grib ridge that our walk follows. It is, like most hill forts, Iron Age, that is early Celtic dating from pre-Roman times. The forts went through a succession of clearly defined steps in the evolution of their defences. At first the natural defences might be augmented by a ditch and rampart, but later, when the attackers were armed with sling shots, there was a

# WALK 26   WAUN FACH

need to keep them further back and more ditches and ramparts were required. Here at Castell Dinas two huge ramparts were constructed at points where the naturally defensive steepness of the spur needed reinforcing. The fort's gate was at the northern end, though there is evidence of a second gate at the south-west.

A thousand years after the earliest occupation the Normans needed to hold the Rhian-goll valley in order to control access to the Usk valley, their main thoroughfare in this part of Wales. At first they constructed a motte within the ramparts of Castell Dinas, before moving down the valley to Tretower.

## Walk 27 Table Mountain

This is the second of the walks that explore the finest of the Black Mountains' ridges. It also has the advantage of visiting Table Mountain, the curious truncated peak that dominates the view of the range from Crickhowell and other nearby spots in the Usk valley.

*Walk category* : Difficult (5 hours).

*Length* : 18 km (11$^1/_4$ miles).

*Ascent* :  680 m (2250 ft).

*Maps* :  Landranger Sheet 161; Outdoor Leisure Sheet 13 Brecon
                Beacons Eastern  Area.

*Starting and finishing point* : The village of Llanbedr, reached by minor roads from Crickhowell or Glangrwyne on the A40 Abergavenny to Brecon road. Beside the village church there is room for a small number of cars. Please park carefully and tidily.

From the church (see (1) Llanbedr) take the lane going north beside the public house to a T-junction of lanes. There go right and follow the lane for about 2 km (1$^1/_4$ miles) to where it doubles back on itself as it crosses a stream. After another 300 m go left up a lane to Neuadd Fawr Farm

WALK 27 ___ TABLE MOUNTAIN

600m

550m

500m

PEN
UT-MAWR
(719m)

650m

700m

450m

400m

350m

S

CWM
BANW

G

300m

650m

250m

NEUADD
FAWR

650m

700m

PEN
CERRIG-CALCH
(701m) ②

650m

600m

250m

550m

500m

450m

N

350m   250m
400m   300m

G   S   G   G
        S   G

TABLE
MOUNTAIN ③

200m

LLANBED
①

S

½        1 Km

½m

and follow the now waymarked lane to a gate. Go through and continue to another gate and stile at the edge of the hillside. Beyond, a path rises past an old quarry, taking a ridge that is a spur of the main ridge. The spur forms the eastern edge of Cwm Banw, and after visiting the top of Pentwynglas where our spur ends, we follow the broad main ridge around the head of Cwm Banw. The main ridge here is flat as well as broad, but it rears up steeply to reach the summit of Pen Allt-mawr.

Ahead the ridge is again broad, though now it gently descends as we follow it southward. About 1 km ($^1/_2$ mile) south of Pen Allt-mawr it splits into two broad ridges. The rightward one – Pen Gloch-y-Pibwr – is only a spur and rapidly ends in a descent to the Rhian-goll valley. Our walk takes the left ridge, which heads south-east and down to a shallow pass. Ahead now is the broad shallow peak of Pen Cerrig-calch (see (2) Pen Cerrig-calch).

From the summit of Pen Cerrig-calch a path heads off south-east towards the as-yet-unseen Table Mountain. When that peak does at last come into view, it is a bit disappointing as it is nothing like as eye-catching as it appears from the valleys. Proceed towards Table Mountain with caution – I was once almost annihilated by a mountain bike near here. The peak (see (3) Table Mountain) itself is an interesting place being much more tilted than is apparent from below, and offering superb views of the Usk valley. To continue go east – most walkers will actually exit from the hill fort on the peak by going back northward and then make their way around to the east side – to reach a path that goes down through a gate to a gate and stile. Beyond is a track that is followed past another gate and stile to the road. Go right, taking the first lane to the left and following that back to Llanbedr.

## (1) *Llanbedr*

The earliest church at the village was consecrated in 1060 and it is believed that part of this still exists as the nave, though that was widened in the sixteenth century. The tower is older, being a fourteenth-century addition to the original building and constructed at a time when the Normans were keen on building towers as much as places of refuge as to satisfy more spiritual needs. Inside, the church has some interesting pieces while outside the lych gate and the yew trees are excellent.

Going in the opposite direction from our Walk the visitor will reach a superb pack-horse bridge over the Gwryne Fechan. The bridge has not been precisely dated, but is certainly medieval.

(2) *Pen Cerrig-calch*

From the Usk valley, on sunny days, a patch of white sparkles on the top of Pen Cerrig-calch making many visitors wonder, especially in winter, whether there is snow on the peak. The walker will find that what sparkles is not snow, but limestone. The Old Red Sandstone that is such a feature of the Black Mountains – as well as of the other hills of the National Park – was laid down in the geological period known as the Devonian which ended about 345 million years ago. Following that, sheets of limestone were laid down during the Carboniferous period. These were overlain by Millstone Grit before the period ended about 280 million years ago. The tilt of the land allowed weathering to begin early on the northern slopes so that whereas on Walk 24 we saw limestone with its quarries and caves and visited a pool on impermeable Millstone Grit, on walks on the Black Mountains the walker expects to find only the Old Red Sandstone, the younger rocks having completely weathered away. Pen Cerrig-calch has a few remaining feet of the original overlying limestone sheet still intact.

The peak's name is interesting. It means Peak of the Limestone Rocks and indicates that the early Welsh farmers, though they might not have understood the geological processes that gave rise to the white rock sheet, certainly understood their area well enough to recognise its existence.

(3) *Table Mountain*

Table Mountain is a typical hill fort in a wonderfully defensive position with commanding views over the Usk valley. As with Castell Dinas (see Note (2) of Walk 26) the natural defences of the site have been supplemented by ramparts. On all sides – if sides is the right descriptive word for a fort that is essentially circular – there are two ramparts, while in the obviously weaker areas the number of ramparts has been increased to four. The Welsh name for the peak, more properly for the fort itself, is Crug Hywel, Hywel's Fort. By tradition the Hywel of the name is Hywel Dda, Hywel the Good. Hywel was a Welsh king of the tenth century, so strictly the fort pre-dates him by a thousand years, but the site is so obviously excellent strategically that there is no reason to believe that a later Welsh king operating before the age of castles would not have occupied the site.

Hywel is an interesting man. He is usually written of as the first Welsh king to have united Wales into one kingdom, though that he did not do, for although he ruled Gwynedd, Powys and Dyfed he failed to secure Gwent and Glamorgan. He is termed 'the Good' for his codification of Welsh law which gave certain legal rights to his subjects. As an example, the laws gave women equal property rights with men, a very forward-looking piece of legislation. The laws also laid down certain requirements and definitions which meant that the common man was not forever at the mercy of merchants. Some of the definitions are eccentric, but great fun. A good mouser cat was worth a sheep, and gold plate must be 'as thick as the nail of a ploughman who has been a ploughman for seven years'. Hywel also laid down the duties of some of the royal household for the first time. These are also interesting, and equally good fun. There was even a Royal Footholder who sat under the king's table to scratch the royal foot when required!

Crug Hywel has given its name to Crickhowell, the fine town on the Usk that stands at the base of the peak. When the Normans came they placed their castle here rather than on the peak and its remains can still be visited. They stand beside one of the nicest village cricket grounds in South Wales. The castle was built by a governor with the unlikely name of Sir Grimbaud Pauncefoot. Perhaps in deference to this name the castle is known as Alisby's Castle after a later owner. While in the town do visit the Usk Bridge a fine early eighteenth-century construction with twelve arches on one side and thirteen on the other. Just outside Crickhowell at Gwernvale, in a building that is now a hotel, Sir George Everest after whom the world's highest mountain is named, was born.

## Walk 28 The Grwyne Fawr Valley

On the eastern side the Black Mountains' ridges define two ribbon-like valleys. The wider of these is the more easterly, the one taken by Walk 29. The valley of the Grwyne Fawr is tighter. In its upper reaches it is heavily afforested and though the stream flows through some very pretty mixed moorland – and is the haunt of the dipper, that most delightful of water birds – the walking is short or too often lost in the trees. Where the trees end however there is a delightful stretch of valley, and a fine walk links the two eastern valleys, a small hamlet, a rare and fascinating old church and a stone linked to an old Welsh legend.

*Walk category* : Intermediate ($4^1/_2$ hours).

*Length* : 12 km ($7^1/_2$ miles).

*Ascent* :  500 m (1650 ft).

*Maps* :  Landranger Sheet 161; Outdoor Leisure Sheet 13 Brecon Beacons Eastern Area.

*Starting and finishing point* : The village of Cwmyoy reached from the road that runs from Llanvihangel Crucorney – on the A465 north of Abergavenny – to Hay-on-Wye by way of the Afon Honddu's valley, known as the Vale of Ewyas, and Gospel Pass. There is very limited car-parking below the church. Please park carefully and tidily.

From the church (see (1) Cwmyoy) follow the village road down past Cwmyoy Farm to reach a signed footpath at the second gate to the right. Go across the field with the fence on your right hand to a footbridge over the Afon Honddu. Go up, crossing a stile to reach the road. Go over the road and up the lane to Coed Farm, going through the farm and up left into the forest. Cross a forest road, continuing left and up to reach the forest edge. Here go across a field to a wall and over it, by a stile, to an open ridge. Go left, following the wall for about 100 m to reach a track going right. Follow this to a lane. Turn left on this and follow it all the way to the bottom of the Grwyne Fawr valley at Five-Ways, a noted local landmark.

   Take the Crickhowell road, the one going west, and cross Pont-yr-Esgob (see (2) Pont-yr-Esgob). Go up to a Y-junction and there go through the gate to the right. Follow a track across two fields to a gate near a ruined farmhouse. Turn half-right and cross the field, turning left at its boundary hedge to follow the hedge to a lane. Go right on the lane and follow it to a sharp right-hand bend. To the right here is Ffynnon Ishow (see (3) Partrishow church), set back a little from the road. Go around the sharp bend to reach the path for Partrishow church (see, also, Note (3)).

After spending time in the church – and Partrishow church is worth all the time you can spare – continue through the churchyard to reach a path which is followed down to Ty'n-y-llwyn Farm. Go through the farm and down a track to the road. Go left and after about 70 m right to a bridge over the Grwyne Fawr river. Take the left fork at a Y-junction, going past the Tabernacle Chapel, and follow the lane past two farms, Ty-mawr and Upper House to a gate on to the hillside. Go through and follow the wall, right, to the Dial Carreg memorial (see (4) Dial Carreg).

Continue on the obvious track past Dial Carreg to where a zig-zag path goes ahead, dropping down into the Honddu valley. That path can be followed, but a more satisfactory route is to bear right with the track that eventually leads to the outward route. Before it is reached, however, a gate left gives access to the forest. Go along the track to reach a forest road. Here go left and almost immediately right on another track. At a fallen tree that blocks the track go left on a path that reaches a fence and stile. Go over and turn half right, going down across the field to a gate on to a lane. Go left and right after 50 m on a lane back to Cwmyoy.

### (1) *Cwmyoy*

Cwmyoy means the Valley – or, more correctly, the Cwm, that is a valley with a headwall – of the Yoke. With a little imagination it is possible to see that the valley is yoke-shaped, though it is nowhere near as obvious as the name would imply. The Church of St Martin is medieval and is curious in having not one square in its construction. This seems more likely to be because of the shape of the bed rock, and its occasional subsidence, than because of incompetent builders. The medieval cross in the church has a curious history. It was discovered at a local farm in the late nineteenth century but disappeared from the church tower in 1967. A photograph of it was shown to the Keeper of Statuary at the British Museum, who dated it to the thirteenth century and remembered that he had recently seen it in a nearby antiques shop. The cross was repossessed and brought back to Cwmyoy.

(2) *Pont-yr-Esgob*

On the first series of the Ordnance Survey's Outdoor Leisure Sheet to the Black Mountains the bridge or, more correctly, the house near it is marked as Pontysbig. On the newest series the name is rendered as Pontyspig. On both sheets a nearby mill was marked as Pont Esgob. Each of these is a misrepresentation, the last a near-miss at least, of Pont-yr-Esgob, the Bishop's Bridge.

The bridge is named for Archbishop Baldwin, the travelling

companion of Gerald of Wales. In truth, of course, the reverse is true since Gerald, a Welsh Norman born at Manorbier Castle in Pembrokeshire, was Archdeacon of Brecon and so of considerably lower rank than his illustrious companion. The two travelled around Wales in 1188 in an effort to win support for the Third Crusade, and Archbishop Baldwin must have made a considerable impact on the locals for them to have named a bridge for him. Gerald was a man of breeding, an intellectual with a flair for writing and a penchant for a colourful legend. He spent his life trying to persuade the Establishment to appoint him Bishop of St David's. Though only one-quarter Welsh, Gerald had a great feel for the country and wished to be Bishop of St David's so that he could then persuade the Pope to confirm him as Archbishop of Wales, a position, he hoped, that would free the Welsh Church from the supremacy of Canterbury. His persuasions were in vain and he never achieved his dream, dying a forgotten man in the early thirteenth century. Gerald might never have been much remembered but for his description of his journey with Archbishop Baldwin. Strangely Gerald does not mention Pont-yr-Esgob or even Partrishow despite its legendary hermit, but he does mention the murder at Dial Carreg (see Note (4) below) and was probably sufficiently nervous about the area just to be glad to be away from it.

(3) *Partrishow church*

Ffynnon Ishow is the Holy Well of St Ishow, a Celtic hermit and mystic who lived in a solitary monastic cell near the spring here on the side of the Grwyne Fawr valley. He showed kindness and hospitality to any traveller and always attempted to persuade them to a Christian way of life. One day a traveller murdered him for his possessions, a pitiful collection. Years later a rich lady who had contracted leprosy on a journey to Europe stopped to drink from the spring and was cured. She gave money for the building of the well house that still survives and for an early church to Ishow.

Partrishow church is remote, and this very remoteness means that its interior has survived Puritans and restorers and is a treasure house of medieval art, despite its plain exterior. The font is huge and is certainly

Cwmyoy church

the oldest item in the church, being inscribed as having been made in the name of Genillin, a pre-Norman Powys prince. On the west wall is a superb mural, a 'doom figure', Father Time painted as a skeleton with dagger, spade and hour glass. Its position, near the church exit, was a reminder to the departing congregation of their mortality. There are three stone altars, two of which have five consecration crosses – one for each of Christ's wounds – a most remarkable survival of the Elizabethan edict that such altars be destroyed and replaced with tables. The third altar is locked in a side chapel and has six rather than five consecration crosses, a strange number.

The finest piece in the church is the rood screen. These screens were common when there was a gallery with musicians to play at services, the rood being a crucifix attached to the front of the screen. Originally the screen would have extended to the floor, another of its functions having been to stop the congregation's dogs from fouling the altar! The screen at Partrishow is almost complete and is now considered a masterpiece of medieval carving. The carving is a continuous dragon and vine theme, with, probably, the dragon representing evil and the vine representing good. The dragon consumes the vine, but good, as represented in the original by the rood itself, always remained on top. It is often said that the artist was Italian or influenced by Italianate art, but this seems to derive from the idea that no medieval Welshman could have carved a vine!

## (4) *Dial Carreg*

Dial Carreg is the Stone of Revenge erected, legend has it, to commemorate the murder of Richard de Clare, a murder mentioned by Gerald of Wales (see Note (2) above) and one which made him nervous. De Clare was on his way home to Cardigan after being involved in several skirmishes with the Welsh on behalf of local Marcher lords. The local lord was with him as guide and protector, but de Clare was an arrogant man and not only dismissed him but sent a singer and fiddler ahead of his small group to announce his coming. The party was ambushed and put to the sword. It is not clear where the attack took place, Gerald referring to the spot merely as Grwyne Wood. Nor is this

Doom figure, Partrishow church

stone original as there was almost certainly a previous one, a larger specimen. Neither is it known who erected the earlier one. To compound the mystery some suggest that the name is not *dial* (revenge), but *deial* (dial) and that the stone was simply a marker on a drove route to the Gospel Pass. As *dial* and *deial* have almost identical pronunciations there is no way of telling now whether the truth is murder or cattle.

## Walk 29 Llanthony Priory

The Afon Honddu flows through a beautiful wide valley, known as the Vale of Ewyas, from close to Gospel Pass – named from a Welsh legend that St Peter and St Paul came this way in answer to a request from the daughter of Caratacus that they preach the gospel to her people – down to the River Monnow and on into the Wye at Monmouth. The eastern ridge of the Vale is the most easterly of the Black Mountains and is taken by the Offa's Dyke long-distance footpath. The western ridge separates the Vale from the valley of the Grwyne Fawr and offers a fine walk with excellent views of the remains of Llanthony Priory, a romantic ruin beautifully set half-way up the Vale.

*Walk Category* : Difficult ($4^1/_2$ hours).

*Length* : 16 km (10 miles).

*Ascent* : 430 m (1400 ft).

*Maps* : Landranger Sheet 161; Outdoor Leisure sheet 13 Brecon Beacons Eastern Area.

*Starting and finishing point* : The car-park beside the ruins of Llanthony Priory on the road through the Vale of Ewyas which runs from Llanvihangel Crucorney, on the A465 north of Abergavenny, to Hay-on-Wye.

From the car-park go back past the church (see (1) Llanthony church) to the entrance and back down to the Vale road and turn right (north) along it. Pass the inn, left, to reach – after about 400 m – a lane to the right. Follow this to its end at a gate. To the right here, but hidden from immediate view, is Siarpol, now a ruin, but once owned by Walter Savage Landor, the poet, whose name is also associated with Llanthony Priory (see (2) Walter Savage Landor).

Beyond the gate the lane becomes a footpath, but continues in obvious style to another gate, beyond which – to keep the walker guessing – it becomes a lane once more. The lane is followed to Garn Farm which is entered and exited through gates, and continues through several more gates before fording a stream and reaching a footbridge over the Afon Honddu. At the lane go right to Capel-y-ffin, too small even to be a hamlet. At a Y-junction go left, leaving the Vale road for a no-through road heading for a small cwm. At the junction the church of St Mary is worth a visit : it stands beside a Baptist chapel, and within a few kilometres of not one but two monastic houses (see (3) St Mary's Church, Capel-y-ffin).

The first of these houses was Llanthony Priory, where our walk started. The second is now to our left, Llanthony Monastery. Though no longer a monastery it is still an impressive monument to one man's faith (see (4) Llanthony Monastery). Beyond the monastery, and about 400 m from the Y-junction, is a signed path going left (west) past the Grange, a riding and trekking centre. Beyond the centre is a gate that gives access to the open country of the Black Mountains.

Ahead now, follow the obvious path that zig-zags up gently towards the obvious steep scarp slope ahead. The scarp is very much steeper, the walker's only compensation for the next 100 m  (320 ft) zig-zag climb being that when it is completed he has halved the climb to the ridge. From the top of the scarp the path rises more gently, reaching the ridge back near a prominent stone known as The Blacksmith's Anvil. Go left (south) along the ridge as it gently rises and falls towards Bâl Mawr's trig point. To the right (west) the view is impeded somewhat by the forestry plantations, but the view left (east) into and over the Vale of Ewyas is excellent. The easterly ridge is the final Black Mountains ridge, and is taken by the Offa's Dyke long-distance footpath.

From Bâl Mawr's trig point the path drops down south-east, joining

THE GRANGE

CHAPEL-Y-FFIN

THE MONASTERY
④

350m
400m
450m
500m
550m
600m

FOOTBRIDGE

THE VISION
OLD SHED

GARN FARM
300m

650m

CHWAREL Y FAN

650m

N

②

250m

600m

⑤  LLANTHO
⑤  PRIOR
①  ⑤

FOOTBRI

250m
300m
350m
400m
450m
500m

CWM BWCHEL

½    1 Km
½m

BÂL MAWR
(607m)    550m

another that has contoured the ridge at a lower level in its journey along the Vale. The obvious path north-east is our route, and is followed down the northern side of Cwm Bwchel, ignoring other paths that head off back up the Vale. Two stiles give access to Cwm Bwchel Farm, beyond which gates lead to a footbridge over the Cwm Bwchel stream which is heading down, as we are, for the Afon Honddu. The Honddu is crossed by a footbridge reached after a wide collection of stiles and gates have been passed, and the path then swings right around a farm to a final gate before the Vale road is reached. Go across the road to reach the lane for the car-park and Llanthony Priory (see (5) Llanthony Priory).

### (1) *Llanthony Church*

The village name is a shortened form of Llan Dewi Nant Honddu, St David's Church by the Honddu Stream, because legend has it that St David spent part of his early life here, the first church having been raised on the site of his monastic cell. The Church of St David that occupies the site today is twelfth-century and was built so that the altar faces the sun as it rises on the saint's day, 1 March. When the Priory was built the church did not serve as priory church, but became a hospital for both the monks and the local folk. When the dissolution came St David's became the parish church again.

### (2) *Walter Savage Landor*

Walter Savage Landor, eccentric and poet, was born in 1775 and was first noted for his eccentricity in 1794 when, as a student at Oxford, he allegedly shot at someone with whose reactionary views he had disagreed. His poetry debut waited four more years, for the publication in 1798 of *Gebir*. Later works were admired for their style and uncompromising ideals, though the romantic nature of much of the work is at odds with the fact that Landor eventually fell out with just about everyone he met and acquired a reputation as a bad-tempered man. He bought the Llanthony estate, including the Priory ruin and a good part of the Vale of Ewyas, in the early nineteenth century, at first living in that part of the Priory which is now an hotel but was then the previous owners' shooting lodge. Landor tried a social and agricultural experiment in the Vale, planting – so it is said – 10,000 trees and importing Spanish sheep. Sadly his anti-social habits and lack of agricultural knowledge doomed the project and he left the area, in part to avoid the enemies that his schemes had created for him. He left behind a poem about the place that begins 'Llanthony! An ungenial clime' and ends 'For never is the heart so true; As bidding what we love adieu'. If he was not attempting to be ironic the effect is to exemplify the contradictions of the man. These are nowhere better shown than in his more famous poem:

> I strove with none, for none was worth my strife;
> Nature I loved, and, next to Nature, Art;
> I warmed both hands before the fire of life;
> It sinks, and I am ready to depart".

It is a lonely piece, the first line of which would have had many a local smarting with indignation.

### (3) *St Mary's Church, Capel-y-ffin*

This beautiful little church should not be missed. It has a delightful gallery running along its south and west walls, and stained glass windows which, upon closer examination, are revealed as being of coloured paper rather than coloured glass.

### (4) *Llanthony Monastery*

Joseph Leycester Lyne was born in Essex in 1837 and ordained as a deacon of the Anglican Church in 1860. Shortly after, he came here because he felt that there was a need to re-establish a monastic (Benedictine) way of life in the Anglican Church. For the rest of his life he lectured in both Britain and America to earn money to build his Llanthony Tertia (see Note (5) below) as he occasionally called the monastery. Lyne styled himself Father Ignatius and was ordained in his monastery in 1898, when he finally accepted that he would not receive the full support of the Anglican Establishment. He was a saintly if obsessive man, a man of 'gently simple kind manners' according to Francis Kilvert, the diarist, who met him in the early years of his work at Llanthony.

The monastery was not finished in Lyne's lifetime, and after his death, in 1908, it began to fall into disrepair, despite the fleeting fame it achieved when it was claimed that a labourer killed during its construction had been restored to life. Ultimately, in 1924, it was bought by Eric Gill, the engraver and sculptor, and is still owned by his family.

### (5) *Llanthony Priory*

One day in the final years of the eleventh century a Norman knight, William de Lacy, was riding through the Vale of Ewyas on a hunting trip. Legend has it that de Lacy was weary of war and strife, but whether that was true or not, when he found the remains of St David's cell at

Llanthony he recognised the spot as holy and determined to stay for the rest of his life, and to raise an abbey. A monk of the Priory was later to write that William 'laid aside his belt...[and] fine linen... The suit of armour, which before defended him from the darts of his enemies, he still wore as a garment to harden him against the soft temptations of his old enemy, Satan ... and continued this hard armour on his body until it was worn out with rust and age.'

Gerald of Wales writes lovingly of the Priory, his account being so much 'first- hand' that many have suggested that he may have spent time there. He recalls a legend of its construction, that the surrounding land was covered with block of marble, 'commonly called free-stones, because they are easily split and can be polished with iron tools. The church is built of them and very attractive they make it. They have this remarkable property, that you can search until you are quite exhausted and collect all these free-stones, until none is left and no more could possibly be found, and then, three or four days later, you can look again and there they all are, just as numerous as before, easy to find if you look and there for you to take'. He also recalls that after Roger, Bishop of Salisbury and right-hand man of Henry I, had visited the site he reported that the king's entire treasure could not build a nave as grand as that offered by the surrounding hills.

Despite the tranquil beauty, however, all was not well. In 1136 a local dispute between Welsh clans resulted in the Priory being besieged for a time and the monks were granted permission to leave Llanthony Priory and construct a daughter house – Llanthony Secunde – on the banks of the Severn near Gloucester. The names here, the first and second Llanthony houses, explain why Father Ignatius called his monastery Llanthony Tertia, the third house (see Note (4) above). Very soon the new house had replaced the old. Gerald, who saw the early stages of this replacement, was appalled. Llanthony – the original Priory that is – 'was formerly a happy, a delightful spot, most suited to the life of contemplation, a place from its first founding fruitful and to itself sufficient. Once it was free, but it has since been reduced to servitude, through the boundless extravagance of the English, its own reputation for rich living, uncontrolled ambition, the ever-growing vice of ingratitude, the negligence of its prelates and its patrons and, far worse than all of these, the fact that the daughter house, become a step-mother, has odiously and enviously supplanted its own mother'. It is difficult to imagine a more eloquently appalled paragraph than that. Gerald went on to describe the deaths of some of the negligent prelates – Prior William was expelled as unworthy, Prior Clement died of a paralytic stroke and Prior Roger (who stole things from the abbey, Gerald says) died a lingering death.

Of course in Secunda itself they saw it differently. Prima was referred to as the prison. One monk asked who would choose to go and sing to the wolves. Gerald would doubtless be pleased to know that many now come to Prima to marvel at the ruins at the Vale, while of Secunda almost nothing at all remains.

Following the founding of the Severnside house, the Priory here was almost entirely de-populated, the number of monks falling to just five at one stage. The Priory also fell on very hard times and was almost impoverished when it was dissolved by Henry VIII. Today it is a magnificently sited, imposing ruin. It is also one of the few places I know where 'wild' gooseberries grow.

Llanthony Priory

# Abergavenny

Though not actually within the boundaries of the Brecon Beacons National Park, Abergavenny is often referred to as the Gateway to the Park. In a sense this is true, as its position in the Usk valley, close to the start of the Heads of the Valleys roads, means that most travellers to the Park from the south or west go close to the town.

Abergavenny is a fine old town, its name causing consternation among many who claim to know a little of the Welsh language. *Aber*, they say with confidence, means a river mouth, as in Aberystwyth and Aberdyfi. Unfortunately for that theory Abergavenny is a long way from the sea. In fact, *aber* means confluence and while that normally means of a river with the sea, here it means of two rivers. The town is actually named for the smaller of the rivers, the Gavenny stream joining the Usk close to the town.

The Normans fortified the town because of its strategic importance: here the Usk river flowed out of its mountain cradle into a broad plain. The castle was held, at an early stage, by William de Braose, a man with a flair for treachery and cruelty, whose murder of a local Welsh chief and his men in the castle after he had invited them to be his guests caused an outrage. Within a year the Welsh had avenged the deaths of their kinsmen by capturing and razing the castle. After this de Braose quarrelled with King John and fled to France. The king imprisoned de Braose's wife and son in Windsor Castle, sending word that they would die of starvation unless he returned. But de Braose did not come, and mother and child both died. It is a sad story, out of which neither the king nor de Braose emerges with much honour.

A walk around the town will reward the visitor, there being a fine old section with many interesting buildings. Be sure to visit the church where there are tombs to members of the de Braose family and a superb Jesse tree carved from a single 3 m (10 ft) piece of oak. Such trees were not uncommon, the reclining figure of Jesse, father of David, holding an Old Testament family tree. The Abergavenny figure is special because of its size and exquisite carving, and for being produced from a single trunk. Nothing now remains of the tree itself, though the roots can still be seen in Jesse's left hand.

## Walk 30 Skirrid Mountain

Abergavenny is dominated by two peaks. To the west is Sugar Loaf, an elegant, conical peak named for its shape. It ought to be the Best Walk in this small area around the town, but it is scarred by paths and occasionally overrun by scrambler motor bikes to such an extent that no sensitive walker could feel happy on its flanks. Skirrid – the name is an Anglicised version of the Welsh name, Ysgyryd Fawr, a name probably deriving from its deep cleft – is a lower peak, a full 100 m (330 ft) lower, and less elegantly shaped. It is, however, a less-trekked peak, has a more interesting tale to tell, and commands a fine view because of its position as the last outline of the eastern Black Mountains.

*Walk Category* : Easy (2 hours).

*Length* : 6 km ($3^3/_4$ miles).

*Ascent* : 300 m (975 ft).

*Maps* :  Landranger Sheet 161; Outdoor Leisure Sheet 13 Brecon Beacons Eastern Area.

*Starting and finishing point* : The car-park at 329 164 at the base of the hill. This is reached by taking the B4521 road eastward out of Abergavenny, towards Skenfrith. The car-park is on the left (north) side of the road.

From the car-park go west, back towards Abergavenny, for a few metres to reach a stile and a signed path that leads northward towards the hill. Another stile leads  to a steep, occasionally stepped path that is followed to a wall crossed by a stone stile. Beyond the wall, the hill is National Trust property.

Go right along the wall for about 80 m to reach an obvious path going left to reach the ridge. Follow the ridge to the trig point and summit (see (1) Ysgyryd Fawr). To return it is necessary to descend the north side of the hill, which is steep in places. Return can be made by going east or west. For those going east – a route which keeps to the wall along its length and offers good views out over the Monmouthshire countryside – an easier descent is down the path heading north-east that starts from the ridge about 50 m south of the trig point. Those going west follow a route through enclosed woodland, which cuts out all long views, but does offer some good short-range ones. Either route follows obvious paths to reach the stone stile of the outward journey. To return to the car-park the outward journey is reversed from here.

## (1) *Ysgyryd Fawr*

Skirrid has long been termed the Holy Mountain, and the summit area still shows some remains of a medieval church to St Michael, built when the hill was a minor pilgrimage centre. The holiness derived from the curious cleft in the hill's otherwise smooth ridge. The cleft is actually the result of a huge landslip but legends grew up around its formation. One story had the hill being rent apart at the time of the Crucifixion, while another placed the cleft earlier, maintaining that it was formed when Noah's Ark landed on the hill as the waters of the flood receded. The soil of the hill was also believed to be holy, some saying that it had been brought from the Holy Land itself, others that St. Patrick had brought it from Ireland. Local farmers collected the soil to sprinkle on their own land, to protect against crop failure.

The church was used before the Reformation, the mass said there on Michaelmas being especially important. After the Reformation, when Catholics were persecuted, secret masses were said in the church, but this is a weatherswept site and the inability of the local Catholics to carry out repairs meant that the church rapidly became ruinous and fell down.

North from the hill is Llanvihangel Crucorney, perhaps the most romantically named village in the area. From the hill the Elizabethan Llanvihangel Court, which lies to the east of the main A465 through the village, can be picked out. The village contains Wales's oldest inn, *The Skirrid*, whose inn sign is the Holy Mountain itself, being struck by cliff-producing lightning. The inn is architecturally very interesting, and worth a visit to quench a walk-induced thirst. If you are tempted to stay, be warned, the inn is haunted. Following the Monmouth rebellion Judge Jefferies led a Bloody Assize here, those who were sentenced to death being held in a small room half way up the stairs before being hanged from a beam above the stairwell. The slab at the bottom of the stairs is reputedly where the hanged bodies were laid out ready for removal and burial. The ghost of the inn is said to be of one of the hanged men.

## Walk 31 The Monmouthshire and Brecon Canal

Between the base of the scarp slope on the southern side of the Usk valley and the river itself lies the Monmouthshire and Brecon Canal, a navigation from the Golden Age of canals. With the coming of the railways the canal, like most others, fell into disrepair, but it has been lovingly restored to provide a fine recreational waterway that is also a linear nature reserve. Close to Abergavenny is one of the finest sections in the canal's length, and it is that section our walk visits.

*Walk category* : Easy ($1^3/_4$ hours).

*Length* : 7 km ($4^1/_2$ miles).

*Ascent* :  60 m (200 ft).

*Maps* :  Landranger Sheet 161; Outdoor Leisure Sheet 13, Brecon Beacons Eastern Area.

*Starting and finishing point* : At the car-park 262 135 in Govilon, beside the old railway line. Govilon is reached along the B4246 that links Llanfoist, just the other side of the Usk from Abergavenny, to a roundabout on the A465 Heads of the Valleys road. Go left on reaching Govilon on a minor road that crosses the canal. Take the right fork at the Y-junction just over the canal and the car-park is 400 m along on the left-hand side.

At the back of the car-park there is direct access to the old railway (see (1) Abergavenny to Merthyr Railway). Go left (east) along the old track, with the village of Govilon (see (2) Govilon) on your left hand. The old station, you will note, is now a field study centre for schools, while further along an old warehouse on Govilon wharf is now a boat clubhouse. Just beyond, bear left near the Waterways Board Canal Office. The railway crossed three bridges on its way to Llanfoist, our

Inn sign in Llanvihangel Crucorney

The Skirrid

Wales oldest Inn

destination, but only the second is intact. At the site of the first there are steps down the embankment to the road that must be crossed to reach steps up again on the far side. There will be steps at the site of the third bridge too, but as work is not yet completed it may be necessary to scramble down and up the banks. The track itself is occasionally overgrown; although it has been closed for only thirty years the willow and birch trees are impressive, as is the growth of undercover scrub. The old track is maintained as a walking route by the Brecon Beacons National Park, a body that is seriously underfunded.

The old track emerges in the village of Llanfoist, our route going right at the dead end and crossing the B4246 to reach the village church (see (3) Llanfoist). Continue up the lane beside the church, forking right at the top to reach the canal (see (4) The Monmouthshire and Brecon Canal). This section of the walk follows the Usk Valley Walk. Turn right (west) along the towpath and follow it to a bridge which is used to change banks. In this section the canal is beautifully sited, with the wooded slopes of Blorenge Mountain to one side, and more open country offering views across the Usk valley to the other.

Beyond the bridge the canal passes through a more built-up area as it nears Govilon. Where the old railway – the outward journey – crosses it, leave the towpath to rejoin the track, which is followed back to the start point.

### (1) *Abergavenny to Merthyr Railway*

Following the successful expansion of Govilon (see Note (2) below) two local companies – called, as was common at the time, civic pride in technology and industrialisation being high, the Merthyr, Tredegar and Abergavenny Company and the Newport, Abergavenny and Hereford Company – combined to build a railway to bring coal from the pits at the valley heads above the scarp slope to the canal. The line followed, in part, the route of the earliest tramway, but also involved some civil engineering work that still brings wide-eyed approval from many a visiting engineer today. Near Govilon itself the line climbed an incline of 1 in 34, and a five-mile stretch in the Clydach Gorge, closer to Ebbw Vale and Tredegar, had an average gradient of 1 in 38. Work on the line started in 1858, but had made no great distance before the local

WALK 31 — THE MONMOUTHSHIRE AND BRECON CANAL

GOVILON ②

LLANFOIST ③

TRACK OF OLD RAILWAY ①

CHURCH
75m
100m

CANAL

BLORENGE

100m

125m

½    1 Km

½m

N

companies were bought out by one of the new giants of steam, the London and North-Western Railway Company in 1866. This company pushed the line on to Merthyr Tydfil. The line survived nationalisation, but was reduced to freight only in 1954 and did not survive Dr Beeching's axe in 1958.

For fifteen years the line was left to rot before this small section was bought by Monmouthshire County Council for the National Park Committee to manage. When it is seen what can be achieved with such small resources, it is a tragedy that more ex-lines are not available to the public as footpaths, and that more money is not spent on maintaining a minimal upkeep. The willow trees that now arch over the line are not only superbly elegant, but very attractive to insects, so that the bird life on the line is excellent. Blue, coal, great, long-tailed and marsh tits can all be seen by the lucky visitor, as can several members of the warbler family – most notably the beautiful blackcap. The limestone that was used as infill for the line has produced an excellent collection of lime-loving flowers, and wild strawberries grow in abundance.

(2) *Govilon*

The name Govilon derives from *gefail*, forge, so there must have been ironworks here from the earliest days of the local industry. The industrialisation of the Clydach Gorge, where there were supplies of iron ore and wood for charcoal, meant prosperity for Govilon not as a centre for forging, but because of its position at the base of the scarp. The digging of the scarp base canal (see Note (4) below) meant that the village was the ideal end point for tramways from the gorge. The most impressive of these was that from the Nantyglo ironworks which was completed in 1821. As we have seen above in Note (1), when steam engines replaced the horse-drawn trams, Govilon maintained its importance, in part because the local tramway builders had been far-sighted in their choice of gauges. The Bailey tramway – to Nantyglo – was 4'4", while the continuation to Llanvihangel and Hereford was 3'6". When the railway came the wide embankments on which the tramways were laid were sufficient in most places to carry the new lines.

Following the decline of the Clydach iron industry, the decline of

The Monmouthshire and Brecon Canal near Llanfoist

canal traffic and the axing of the railway, Govilon became a quieter, more peaceful place. Those wishing to gain some insight into the way of life of the people when Govilon, and nearby Llanfoist, were busy industrial centres should read Alexander Cordell's *Rape of a Fair Country* which is set in the villages in the early years of the nineteenth century.

### (3) *Llanfoist*

Llanfoist is another village which grew up and found prosperity as a result of its position. There were limekilns beside the church a century or more ago, the rock being brought down from the Pwll-du Quarry on the west side of Blorenge Mountain by a tramway – the Hills Tramway – that ran through a tunnel for most of the way and crossed the old Tods bridge near where our walk joins the canal.

The village was the birthplace of Captain Thomas James, though he is usually known as Captain James of Bristol or of Blaenafon. James was born in the last years of the sixteenth century and was an impressionable twenty-year-old when Henry Hudson died after being cast adrift when an expedition to find the North-West Passage failed after the discovery of Hudson Bay. James was involved in a later attempt at the Passage and was financed by Charles I on an expedition in 1631 that found and named James Bay. The expedition, which lasted eighteen months, involved appalling hardships which formed the basis for a fine book that James wrote on his return. The book is believed to have been an inspiration to Samuel Taylor Coleridge, though the poet's 'Rime of the Ancient Mariner' was set in more southerly latitudes. Captain James died in 1635.

### (4) *The Monmouthshire and Brecon Canal*

When it was originally built the canal here was called the Brecon and Abergavenny and was built to transport agricultural lime and farm produce as much as to provide a carrier for the developing iron industry in the Clydach Gorge. The building of the waterways during the Golden Age of canals required the setting up of canal companies to survey the route and finance the scheme, and an enabling Act of Parliament to be passed. The Act enabling construction of this canal was passed in 1793, though construction did not start until 1797. In part this was due to the early construction of tramways. The enabling Acts allowed the canal companies to build tramways up to 8 miles from the canal – the 'mileage' – which were very lucrative as usually the company ordered the rolling stock and charged for its use. Local industries could buy and maintain their own rolling stock, but they still had to pay for use of the tramway, so the canal company was keen to avoid competition from rival tramways. The canal took fifteen years to build which, since it is only 52 km (33 miles) long, seems a very long time. In part this was due to its phased construction, firstly from Pontnewydd to the Monmouthshire Canal at Pontymoel near Pontypool, then the Brecon to Abergavenny section and finally the last link. In part it was due to the method of construction, manual digging by navigators, as the labouring men were called. The navigators had only pickaxes, shovels and wheelbarrows and so hard was the work that the shortened version of their name – 'navvies' – is still a term applied to anyone involved in hard, physical labour. The bridges and other engineering works were the responsibility of Thomas Dadford, who also surveyed the route. So good a canal engineer was he that there are only six locks along the canal's length, five of which are in a short section near Llangynidr.

As with all Britain's canals, rail and then road transport made the waterway uncompetitive, and it fell into disrepair. Fortunately the Torfaen Canal Society, together with other interested groups including the Nature Conservancy, have restored much of the canal and it is now a favourite with pleasure-craft owners and wild life. Evidence of the work involved in the upkeep of such a waterway can be seen on our route, about 400 metres west of Llanfoist where a serious bank failure in 1976 has been repaired. Gradually the equilibrium of the wild life at the site of the failure, destroyed at the time of the breach and during repair work, is being restored. Here, and elsewhere along the towpath the walker may see tree-creepers and nuthatches among the trees. The lucky walker may see redpolls feeding among the alders, while the very lucky one may catch sight of a kingfisher. The water itself contains wild life more usually associated with a pond – the canal is, after all, a linear pond. The water plants too are pond plants, with pondweeds and lilies, and reeds and rushes at the margin. Water forget-me-not can also be found, while away from the water there are other fine plants including hemlock-water-dropwort, wall-rue, spleenwort and maidenhair ferns.

# The Valleys

The Millstone Grit that overlies the carboniferous limestone to the south of the Llangattock escarpment, the rim of the Usk valley, is itself overlaid to the south by rocks of the Coal Measures. The Measures are as much as 2000 m (6500 ft) thick in places and consist of a mixture of shale, sandstone and coal seams. The Measures are sub-divided into Upper, Middle and Lower, the Upper giving the area its dune-sloped plateau, while the Middle and Lower are mined for coal. The coal type and quality varies with position. To the east the coal lies at depth, but is high-quality anthracite and steam coal, while to the west it lies closer to the surface – so close that it can be drift mined, that is from horizontal rather than vertical shafts – and is a coking coal. This distribution explains also the distribution of the steel industry, which tended to arise in the west, close to the available coking coal for charging blast furnaces.

Into the thick Coal Measures are cut a number of parallel river valleys each flowing from the north-west to the south-east, to the coastal plain, Cardiff and Newport. These valleys, the Ebbw, the Sirhowy, Rhymney, Taff, Cynon and Rhondda, form the most famous industrial area in Britain, a land of myth and legend. The rivers themselves have a pattern that takes little account of the underlying geology and, indeed, even seems on occasions to run counter to the lie of the land and the geological fault pattern. It has been surmised to explain this that the Measures were once overlaid by a thick layer of chalk and that the rivers took their courses from the geography of this layer, cutting down into the rocks of the Measures as the chalk was eroded. The rivers exposed coal, although weathering of the surface also exposed coal in the north-west around Blaenafon and Ebbw Vale, and this was almost certainly used as a domestic fuel from earliest days. Not until the Industrial Revolution was the coal exploited on a large-scale commercial basis. The production of coking coal helped the iron and steel industries that had developed around the local iron ore deposits, coke replacing charcoal as a fuel, a happy find as supplies of charcoal were becoming scarce as the local forests were cleared. Steam coal from the west drove the trains that came at a later stage to shift both coal and the finished steel, and the ports of Cardiff and Newport expanded rapidly. At the time South Wales was at the forefront of technology: Trevethick laid out the world's first railway between Abercynon and Merthyr Tydfil; in Blaenafon high-quality steel was made for the first time from low-phosphorus iron ore; and near Llantrisant in 1853 Dr William Price cremated his dead son, the first such cremation of modern times.

The valleys are steep-sided, the old villages, built at a time when the population level was higher and the area more prosperous, extending ribbon-like along the sides. In them the heroes are not ancient Celts from Arthurian legend or tales of the *Mabinogion*, but more modern men: the Valleys, the capital V here is deliberate, are a land not of Brochfael the Fanged but of Dai the Fly-Half. The people of the Valleys were a tightly-knit folk, suspicious of outsiders. The dangers of mining produced an enviable community spirit, the conditions of work providing a distrust of apparently well-intentioned non-Valley dwellers.

The Valleys are a playground for the industrial geologist and the social historian, but are less wonderful for the walker, the ribbon development limiting access to the valleys, the mine spoil making life occasionally difficult on the ridges. Here is a place for visiting, not tramping around. Yet to avoid the area altogether is to ignore some of the most significant places both in Wales and in Welsh history. For that reason a slight departure in format is required. Our Best Walk will visit not the country, but a town.

## Walk 32 Blaenafon

Around the 1780 Blaenafon – the Top of the River, the river in this case being the Afon Llwyd – was an area with a few scattered farms, none of them very big, and none of the farmers very prosperous. One hundred years later there were almost 10,000 people living in one of Britain's foremost industrial towns. At around the same time two men working in Blaenafon's ironworks solved a long-outstanding problem in steel making, giving the town new impetus. By the early years of this century Blaenafon had grown to a prosperous town of 13,000 people, The Twenties brought decline, as they did to almost every town in Britain, but in Blaenafon the decline was nearly terminal. Today the town has

WALK 32 BLAENAFON

N

BLAENAFON IRONWORKS

S

TY MAWR

POLICE STATION

WORKMAN'S INSTITUTE

ST. PETER'S CHURCH,

ST. PETER'S SCHOOL

BIG PIT

1/2    1/2    1 Km

fewer then half its peak population and there are large areas of decay and dereliction. Yet within a small area there are some of the finest industrial archaeological sites in Britain, sites which alone would make Blaenafon worth a visit. But there is more here, even if it is less tangible, and for that reason Blaenafon is the pivot point of the Torfaen Museum Trust which has care of many of the important sites in the upper Llwyd Valley. Blaenafon is the essence of South Wales. Here there was a pit and a steel works, they prospered, they declined, they closed. It is a joke that the industries of South Wales close on Friday nights and reopen as museums on Monday mornings, a joke often thought by the locals to be in very bad taste. But we should be grateful for the existence of the museum sites and buildings of Blaenafon, to show how the Valleys used to be.

The walk described here is a short one, through a small section of the town and does not really fit well into the style used for describing the others. Interesting points will therefore be described in the text.

*Walk Category* : Easy (1 hour).

*Length* : 4 km ($2^1/_2$ miles).

*Ascent* : 40 m  (130 ft).

*Maps* :  Landranger Sheet 161; Pathfinder Sheet 1110 (SO 20/30)
               Pontypool and Abertillery (though only the map given with the
               walk is necessary).

*Starting and finishing point* : The Ironworks car-park, well signed from all parts of the town.

The first thing that catches the eye in the car-park (and how could it fail to do so?) is the huge, but modern, steel press. The second is the name of the nearby industrial estate, Gilchrist Thomas. By the mid-nineteenth century the work of Bessemer and Siemens meant that steel had replaced iron as the major constructional metal. Unfortunately, steel could only be produced from low-phosphorus ore, a high phosphorus content making the steel too brittle, and these comprised only about 10 per cent of known ores. The problem of how to use high-phosphorus ore exercised the minds of steel-making chemists for about a quarter of a century. Sidney Gilchrist Thomas, though the son of a Welshman, was a clerk at London's Metropolitan Police Courts and a keen, but amateur, chemist. For years he worked on the problem of high-phosphorus steels with a small furnace in his rooms, eventually persuading his cousin, Percy Gilchrist, the chemist at Blaenafon's ironworks, to help him. The two carried out a series of experiments at the site – Sidney Gilchrist Thomas travelling down at weekends to work – and in 1878 solved the problem by use of a chemically basic slag rather than the acid one in use at the time. After the discovery Thomas – who also had the good sense to realise that the process's high phosphorus residue was useful agriculturally – was feted throughout the world, meeting and selling his patents to Andrew Carnegie. Sadly Thomas failed to receive the full benefit of his fortune, dying at just thirty-five in 1885. The naming of the estate is a fine memorial to the man, though elsewhere in the world his name is held in higher esteem than it is in his own country.

The Ironworks, reached across the road from the car-park and now in the hands of Cadw, was the first to have been built at Blaenafon and dates from 1789. There are five blast furnaces built into the side of the hill so that they could be charged from above, and the superb remains of a balance tower. This was used to transfer pig iron to the tramways on Blorenge Mountain, water being diverted into boxes that, when full, were heavy enough to raise trolleys of iron up the towers. At the tower base the boxes were emptied, the heavier trolleys then hauling them back up. Also on the site are rows of workers' cottages, tiny two-up, two-down terraced cottages. In one of these one ironworker's wife raised nineteen children. The life of the workers was harsh and as the company controlled the only shop there was poverty and resentment.

One target for resentment is seen when we leave the Ironworks. Go left out of the site, down to the T-junction and turn right. The road falls and curves left, and on the left side is Ty Mawr, the Big House, built for one of the Ironworks' owners and contrasting with the tiny cottages at the site. Blorenge Mountain was at the time Britain's most southerly

Steel press, Blaenafon

grouse moor and in season the house would be full of shooting guests. The men in the works, forbidden to join a union even though an employers' association existed to help maximise profits, must have been resentful indeed.

Further on, but to the right, is St Peter's School built by Sarah Hopkins, sister of Samuel, an early works' owner. She built it in 1816 to his memory, adding an inscription, in Latin, that noted her brother's 'benevolent intentions...towards his Glenavonians'. The gesture was a fine one, and the school had 120 pupils when it first opened, but not everyone shared Sarah's opinion of her brother's benevolent intentions. The word Glenavonians is interesting, implying that a non-local carver was used, one who had no idea of the town's name and misread his instructions.

Beyond the school there is a fine building to the left, a police station and courthouse, built in 1867. Opposite it is St Peter's Church, a remarkable building of 1805. The church is a simple structure of local stone but the window frames and sills, the tomb covers and the font are of cast iron. The cast font is a unique feature. Inside there are memorials to the Hopkins and Hill families, the Ironworks' owners, while the churchyard holds the graves of many Midlanders brought here in the early days when there was a shortage of local labour.

The next building to the left is perhaps the finest memorial to the workers of Blaenafon, the Workmen's Hall and Institute. The building, a sturdy, confident structure with just a hint of sensitive decoration, was completed in 1894, paid for by contributions from steelworkers and miners. The building held an auditorium for concerts and shows, a games room and, most remarkable of all, a library and reading room. Sadly the building has decayed, but it is now being worked on and it is to be hoped that it will return to its former glory.

The Hall is a good place to stop, though there are other fine buildings, most notably the Moriah Chapel from 1888 and the earlier Horeb Chapel of 1862, but one more site should be visited. Most people will go by car as the Big Pit Mining Museum is over 2 km ($1\frac{1}{4}$ miles) from the Ironworks. The walk is straightforward enough, but can be depressing.

The winding engine, Big Pit

Big Pit itself, the mine that visitors can descend, was sunk in 1860, but forms part of a complex of coal mines that were first sunk to supply the coal needs of the Blaenafon Ironworks. When the mine finally closed in 1980 it was the oldest working mine in the South Wales coalfield. Today it has a good image and is often alive with the sound of children's laughter. In 1840 a Parliamentary Commission found many of the most crucial functions in the mine being carried out by other children who had little to laugh about. One boy, a veteran of three years in the pit at the age of seven, smoked a pipe all day in order to stay awake. The Commission also found that in 1838 fifty-eight children aged under thirteen had been killed in mine accidents. The Commission tried to have children banned from the mines, an action strongly opposed by the government who claimed that such a move would bring about a collapse of the industry. Ironically enough, when the law was passed and an inspector turned up at Blaenafon to ensure compliance, he was besieged by a crowd of local folk angry at the loss of income to their families.

# The Wye Valley and the Forest of Dean

The Wye is the most beautiful river valley in Britain. From Plynlimon, where the river starts as it means to go on, in a well-defined valley to a point south of Chepstow where it joins the Severn and the sea, the Wye has not one industrial blemish. So unpolluted is the river and so untarnished the countryside it flows through that its whole length has been designated a Site of Special Scientific Interest. In its lower reaches, south from Ross-on-Wye, the river flows in a sometimes high-sided but always deeply wooded valley where over 690 native species of tree and shrub grow. In this area the river is flowing through limestone country, and here it also forms the border between England and Wales. In its upper reaches the river is wholly Welsh, flowing out of the mountains of Plynlimon and into a wooded section south of Builth Wells that is one of its finest sections. From Hay-on-Wye the river's middle section is wholly English, meandering across the Herefordshire plain.

The Wye as a tourist attraction was 'discovered' by the Revd William Gilpin, high priest of the Picturesque – see the introduction to Walk 36 below – with his book *Observations on the River Wye and Several Points in South Wales* published in 1782. Gilpin made a trip down the river and soon the Wye Tour became the thing to do if you had pretensions to being someone in late eighteenth- and early nineteenth-century society. The Wye Tourers were transported by boat, starting from Ross-on-Wye, as the river was deemed unnavigable by boats loaded with gentlefolk north of the town. In a rowing boat equipped with six or eight sturdy locals the Tourers would watch the river go by, sketching perhaps if the mood took them, from under the cover of their protective awning. At suitable times an on-boat or on-shore picnic would be taken, hampers laden with food and wine being brought for the purpose. At the end of Day One, the Tourers would spend the night in Monmouth. On Day Two they would finish their Tour at Chepstow.

Today's Wye tourer must paddle his own canoe, and since the Wye is, from Glasbury to Chepstow, a public river the canoeist can proceed at his leisure. The canoe trip is one of the best ways of seeing the river. It is a gentle, easy enough journey, the only rapids being at Monnington and Symonds Yat and these offering more fun than problems. And if you are alone in early summer, on the river as the sun is rising, with the birds and the damsel flies, it is a fine place to be.

Those keener on seeing the valley than the river at constant close quarters will find it well supplied with walks. In Walk 1, we visited the Wye's source; below we explore the lower reaches.

It seems strange to include an area of England in a book on Wales, but the Forest of Dean has always been a mysterious place, neither England nor Wales, just Dean. Also, since the logical return route of Walk 36 is on the English side of the Wye and in the Forest, it seemed a shame not to include just one Walk that explored this most ancient landscape.

Today the Forest covers 10,900 hectares (27,000 acres), just a fraction of its total area when early man first cleared the trees for his farming. It was later development that reduced the forest's site, the discovery of iron ore in the forest bringing a need for charcoal, the trees being felled in huge numbers to produce it. The Normans checked this destruction by making Dean a Royal Forest, but by the Middle Ages iron-making with charcoal-fired blast furnaces was in full production. Henry VIII realised the importance of the Forest as a supplier of trees for the Royal Navy, but his protection laws fell into disrepute and a seventeenth century iron master, Sir John de Winter, started to destroy trees at an alarming rate. It has been calculated that had it not been for the Civil War de Winter would have felled the forest, converting it *en masse* into charcoal. During the Commonwealth the enormous damage that had been done to the Forest was recognised and trees – mostly oaks – were planted by the thousand. The remaining Forest was fenced to prevent animals from eating seedlings – an action that caused riots among the locals – and slowly recovered. Nelson visited the Forest two years before his death at Trafalgar and his criticism of its state did much to persuade the authorities into a new programme of planting and protection. The Free Miners – men who lived in the Forest and claimed the right to mine coal and iron-ore at any site of their choosing, a right they jealously guarded, passing the freemanship down from father to son – were required to pay for any trees they felled for pit props, and the destruction of trees was halted. It is doubtful though whether the decline in Forest area would have been so easily halted if coking coal had not replaced charcoal in blast furnaces or the iron-clad battleship not replaced the man o'war.

Today the Forest is a mix of the ironically necessary fast-growing conifers and ancient woodland, still mainly oaks. There are small herds of fallow deer – at one time there was an attempt to wipe out the deer stock in order to stop poachers who damaged trees and saplings – and a fine collection of woodland birds.

## Walk 33 Boughrood

After it has left Plynlimon the Wye flows in a deep, but less steep-sided, valley through Llangurig to Rhayader. From there the river is followed by the Upper Wye Valley Walk, a fine route that takes the walker 55 km (35 miles) to Hay-on-Wye. Below Builth Wells the route hugs the river bank in the finest section of river scenery in the early part of the Wye's journey. The route, like the river, is linear rather than circular, but a return is possible using quiet country lanes where the walker is usually alone with the hedgerows.

*Walk Category* : Easy ($2^1/_2$ hours).

*Length* : 10 km ($6^1/_4$ miles).

*Ascent* : 30 m (100 ft).

*Maps* :  Landranger Sheet 161; Pathfinder Sheets 1015 (SO 04/14)
            Aberedw and 1038 (SO 03/13) Talgarth.

*Starting and finishing point* : The village of Llyswen, on the A470 from Builth Wells to Bronllys/Talgarth.

From the village (see (1) Llyswen) go north-west, back towards Builth Wells, for about 500 m and take the road beside the inn signed for Boughrood. The lane to the left passed shortly is where the return route re-enters Llyswen. The Wye is first sighted from the Boughrood Bridge, a real appetiser for the second half of the walk. When Boughrood is reached go left, following the road signed for Painscastle, to the church (see (2) Boughrood). The churchyard offers a change to escape from

WALK 33 BOUGHROOD

ABEREDW

LLANSTEPHAN BRIDGE

LLANSTEPHAN

G

S

G

G

G

VIEWPOINT

G

OAK TREE

S

G

A479

N

LLANGOED CASTLE ③

STANDING STONE

G

G

WATER AUTHORITY BUILDING

½    1 Km

½ m

HOUSE

BOUGHROOD ②

SCHOOL

INN

RIVER WYE

Ⓢ  LLYSWEN

road walking, if only for a few metres. Beyond the church the road doglegs left and right, and then left again as we take a lane north-west towards Llanstephan and Aberedw. The church at Llanstephan is worth a visit, if only for the views from it and the superb yew trees. Aberedw is famous for the part it played in the last days of Llywelyn the Last. A cave among the rocky outcrops above the village is known as Llywelyn's Cave and is reputedly where the last Prince of Wales of Welsh royal lineage spent his final days. From it he rode to Cilmery a little way from Builth Wells, where he was killed by one Adam Francton, an English soldier who had no idea of who it was he had speared. When he was told he returned to cut off Llywelyn's head so that the English king could exhibit it on a spike at the Tower of London, crowned with ivy. Llywelyn's headless body was spirited away, probably to Abbey Cwmhir.

Beyond the lane to Llanstephan, and the turning off to Aberedw, our route crosses Llanstephan Bridge. The bridge is a glorious construction of wood and iron and offers a fine view of the river. To reach the river go left along the verge of the main road for 200 m to a signed path – a yellow arrow on a wooden post, a sign for the Upper Wye Valley Walk – left. Beyond a gate follow the fence to the river and go right (south-east) along it. The bank itself can occasionally be followed, but usually the easiest walking is at the field edge.

This is a superb piece of country. The river itself is at its prettiest and ahead is the striking outline of Mynydd Troed, climbed by Walk 25. In spring the fields are carpeted with bluebells and celandine, the broom is purest yellow and woodpeckers drum away in the trees. A magnificent oak tree is passed just before a stile, beyond which a gate in the fence to the left gives access to a river viewpoint with a seat. A rutted lane gives the way for a few metres and a gate leads to an old wooden hut, a curious concrete slab, a rusting car and a superb avenue of sweet chestnut trees. In addition to other oaks and chestnuts there are birch, hazel, hawthorn, holly, sycamore and, of course, willow. To the right the eye is taken by Llangoed Castle (see (3) Llangoed Castle) and a tall, elegant standing stone.

Beyond a small pier the walk reaches a metalled lane past a pumping station, a lane that is followed to Llyswen. In the final few metres past the school the smell of wild garlic can be overpowering at the right (?) time of the year.

### (1) *Llyswen*

The village is named for a *llys-wen*, a white court, built here in the ninth century by Roderic, a prince of southern Wales. The court was said to have been the finest in the whole of Wales though nothing of it now remains. At the time of Roderic the Celtic Welsh still practised *gavelkind*, the division of a father's land between his sons on his death, a continual source of trouble in Welsh history as the sons fought for total control. Roderic divided his kingdom as equally as he could, and decreed that each son should have a court where disputes between them could be settled amicably. One of these courts was here at Llyswen. After his death, however, the sons forgot all their fine promises and civil war broke out. One victim of the wars was Llyswen which lost not only its court, but its place of importance in Welsh affairs.

Late in the eighteenth century the village was briefly famous again when John Thelwall, the radical who had been tried for sedition, moved into a local farm. There he was visited by William Wordsworth and his sister Dorothy. At that time the poet who was later to become such a pillar of the Establishment was himself a radical young man.

### (2) *Boughrood*

Boughrood has an English-looking name and it comes as a surprise to many visitors to find that it is pronounced 'bock-rue-id', the name actually deriving from the Welsh *bach rhyd*, little ford. The ford here, and, later, the bridge, once carried the visitor between the counties of Breconshire and Radnorshire, before both were swallowed by the new Powys. There are two castles, in the village, one a Norman motte, the other a nineteenth century private house and once occupied by Francis Fowkes. He had fifteen children by a London actress called Mary Lowe, without taking the time to marry her, after returning from making a fortune in India where, legend has it, he had left another fine brood with an Indian woman whom he also forgot to marry.

Boughrood church is Victorian, an earlier church having all but fallen

The Wye near Llyswen

down through neglect. It was mentioned to Francis Kilvert, the famous diarist, who noted that the choir sat on the altar, there being nowhere else, and were accompanied only by a drum. At about the same time a published guide to the local area suggested avoiding the village where there was no fit lodging for a lady, though it did note that the view of the Wye from the bridge was a fine one, and for it 'a venial trespass should be risked'.

### (3) Llangoed Castle

The building is not correctly called a castle, though there is a local story that it does indeed stand on the site of a medieval castle. It dates, in fact, from the early years of this century and is a huge mansion designed by Sir Clough Williams-Ellis who is (rightly) more famous for his Italianate folly village Portmeirion in North Wales. The castle is not open to the public.

## Walk 34 Symonds Yat

When the Wye Tourers left Goodrich Castle with its fine position, its romantic ruins and the ghosts of a young couple who drowned in the Wye beside it as they struggled to escape the twin perils of the Civil War and an irate father, they were treated to two huge, meandering river bends. The first took them 5 river-kilometres (3 miles) to reach Welsh Bicknor about 700 land-metres away. The second was even bigger and it took closer to 7 river-kilometres (about $4^1/_2$ miles) to circumnavigate the 500 metre land neck of Symonds Yat. The Tourers did not stay in the boats here, preferring to climb Yat Rock for the views. Our route also climbs the Rock, after descending through the Forest to reach the Wye and following past its famous section of rapids.

*Walk category* : Easy/Intermediate (2 hours).

*Length* : 8 km (5 miles).

*Ascent* : 180 m (600 feet).

*Maps* : Landranger Sheet 162; Outdoor Leisure Sheet 14 (Wye Valley & Forest of Dean).

*Starting and finishing point* : The Ready Penny picnic site at 569 132 to the left of the B4432 road that links Christchurch with Symonds Yat.

With your back to the road head for the far right corner of the car-park, passing a 'No Through Road' sign for a track into the forest. A yellow arrow gives the line along a narrow, overgrown path to the left, the path being followed through a good section of oak wood to a broad earthy track. A sign here points right to Symonds Yat. Our return route will come from there to here so it is advisable to make a note of the features and sign as the path back to the car-park can be missed. Leftward (south) is signed for Buckstone. We shall not reach this stone, which is at 542 123, but it is worth visiting from the car-park near it at a later stage. It is a logan rock, that is a rock so well-balanced that it can be rocked gently by the slightest pressure. Sadly, vandals in 1885 overturned it and it no longer rocks, but before then its balance was so perfect that even gentle breezes moved it. The rocking of logans was supposed to foretell the future and many legends have grown up around the stone, for example, if you walk three times around it at dawn any wish you make will come true, or that it was a sacrificial stone of the druids.

Follow the track towards the Buckstone almost to a car-park, a few metres short of which a narrower track right (north-west) signed for the River Wye is taken. This track goes down through the Forestry Commission's Highmeadow Woods (see (1) Highmeadow Woods), steeply in places, but always straightforwardly. The only complex part is where a narrow track to the right must be taken off the wide descent track. This narrow track is signed by a waymarking post and is just beyond the overhead power lines. At a junction with a wider track go left to follow a fine stream down to the river (see (2) The Slaughter). The 'official' path now is to go right following the yellow arrows of the Lower Wye Valley Walk. This walk takes a line away from the river, but the bank itself can be walked along virtually its entire length to Symonds Yat (see (3) Symonds Yat).

As the village is neared the impressive Royal Hotel is reached. Leave

WALK 34   SYMONDS YAT

N
↑

RIVER

PANORAMA
DIAL

RSPB
VIEWPOINT
④

100m

STEPS

SYMONDS
YAT ③

ROYAL HOTEL

RAPIDS

FOOTBRIDGE

LONG STONE ④

150m

THE
SLAUGHTER
②

50m

HOUSE

100m

MARKER
POSTS

POWER
LINES

½        1 Km

½m

150m

HIGHMEADOW
WOODS

⑤

200m

the Lower Wye Valley Walk here, going right to the hotel and going left along its wall, passing a castle-like tower. The steep track here is signed for Yat Rock, but is left after about 250 m for an unsigned, stepped path to the right – the first path passed. This path rises very steeply and a path off of it, also on the right, but this time signed for Yat Rock, is equally steep. At the top of this path, which twists and turns upwards, is a Forestry Commission site with car-parking and refreshments, and a footbridge over the main road to Yat Rock (see (4) Yat Rock).

   Retrace the path from the Rock to the car-park, leaving it along a track that runs parallel to the road. This wide track is followed all the way back to the outward lane from the start car park. At a Y-junction take the left fork, at a house go straight ahead, at a crossroads of tracks go straight over, always following the obvious track. At the sign (Buckstone/Symonds Yat) go left along the narrow outward track to the car-park.

(1) *Highmeadow Woods*
The Forestry Commission's Highmeadow Woods cover 1400 hectares (3500 acres) and are a mixed wood with over twenty species of tree including some superb beeches. The wood is also home to one of the last two large herds of fallow deer in the Forest of Dean – the other is in the woods near Speech House – and the lucky visitor may catch sight of them. They are nervous creatures, rarely leaving the full cover of the woods during the day, and are usually seen either at dawn or dusk. The bird life is excellent, with five species of tit, tree-creepers, nuthatches, all three species of the woodpeckers, redstarts, pied flycatchers, wood warblers and even tree pipits. The patient or very lucky visitor may also catch sight of that most elusive forest bird, the hawfinch.

   The woods are part of the ancient Forest and have remained unchanged for centuries. Not surprisingly, therefore, there are mythical sites. At 541 141 is the Suckstone, a huge monolith (single stone), one of the largest in Britain. Estimates of its weight vary, but it could be as much as 4000 tons, which is certainly heavy for a pebble. Close by is Near Harkening Rock, a brother to Far Harkening Rock closer to the river. No satisfactory explanation of the names exists, but they are said to have been used by gamekeepers listening for poachers.

### (2) *The Slaughter*

In the tenth century Eric Bloodaxe, leader of a Viking band, landed at Beachley where the old Aust Ferry also landed after crossing the Severn and close to where the Severn Bridge still touches land on the Welsh side. His band raped and pillaged their way to Symonds Yat, camping there on the protected high land which offered them a clear view of an advancing army. And indeed a Saxon army did come, marching up the Wye in pursuit. The Vikings poured down on the Saxons and in the battle that followed so many were killed that the site of the encounter became known as The Slaughter. Such is one, fairly unlikely, version of how this area of the Wye's left bank came by its name. Another prefers its battle to be between the Romans and retreating Celtic tribesmen under the leadership of Caratacus. On the other bank, and a little to the west, is Little Doward hill fort where the Silures and Ordovices – men from tribes whose names are now used to describe types of rock in the geology of Wales and the world – are said to have camped before the battle. Certainly Caratacus did form an army of Celtic men, and did fight the Romans in South Wales. He was finally betrayed and captured in AD51 and spent the rest of his life as an honoured guest of Rome, but there is no direct evidence of a battle here on the Wye's banks.

Neither of the these stories – nor another, less common one that deals with a Civil War skirmish – seems likely to be responsible for the name. The villages of Upper and Lower Slaughter in the nearby Cotswolds are now believed to derive their name from the Saxon for sloe trees, which would also seem to be a more likely explanation of the name here.

### (3) *Symonds Yat*

Most experts agree that the Yat part of the village's name is derived from *gate*, the Saxon word for a track. About Symonds there is much less agreement. Some would like to see it deriving from *seaman*, to indicate that the village was on an invasion route of the Vikings, a useful tie-up with one derivation of the name, The Slaughter (see Note (2) above). Others have a more prosaic explanation, seeing the name as deriving from Robert Symonds, a seventeenth century High Sheriff of Herefordshire.

The Wye from Symonds Yat

The village is a tourist trap, all ice-creams and boat trips, but is undoubtedly pretty. The old ferry across the Wye – the river divides the village into two parts, the western half being slightly less brash – is interesting, the flat-bottomed boat being man-hauled across by means of an overhead cable.

The rapids in the Wye just south of the village are a favourite spot for canoeists. The natural obstructions in the river (see Note (4) below) have been added to, to form a series of tight channels which offer an exciting, but quite safe, ride.

(4) *Yat Rock*

One Wye Tourer noted that the climb from the river to Yat Rock 'though a work of some toil, will reward the curious observer'. The suggestion was that the Rock was 2000 ft high, a slight (!) exaggeration on the actual height of 500 ft (150 m).

The best explanation for the long gorge that takes the Wye around the Rock is that the long meander was formed when the sea level was around 180 m (600 ft) higher than it is now, and that when the level dropped the river cut down into the rock, leaving behind a raised table of limestone. The upper bands of limestone include one of Lower Dolomite, a band of rock with vertical jointing whose weathering has produced a series of detached towers. The collapse of one helped produce the Wye Rapids, while another has produced Long Stone, the tower of rock, dripping with vegetation, that pokes its way through the trees and is so eye-catching from Symonds Yat. This tower, and the nearby cliffs of Lower Dolomite and Crease Limestone, are favourites with rock climbers.

On the opposite side of the Rock from Long Stone is the famous viewpoint that the Wye Tourers toiled to reach. Today's visitor is assisted in admiring the view by a panorama dial, but it is the Wye that draws the eye, virtually the whole of the meander being visible from here. Here too is an RSPB observation point, a telescope (in season) helping the visitor to a better view of a nest site of a pair of peregrine falcons who have frequented the Rock for several years. These magnificent birds, slate grey and very quick, have been badly persecuted by egg collectors and others seeking young birds for training in falconry, and the Society's protection work at this and other sites is to be

applauded.  A peregrine stooping is one of nature's truly great sights and
it would be a tragedy if it was lost from British skies.

## Walk 35 Forest Sculpture

The Forest of Dean is criss-crossed with paths, and traversed by
unfenced roads. In the sense that this gives almost complete access to the
forest, and because – dare one say it – one tree looks like another, there
is no Best Walk: almost, perhaps, no need for a Best Walk. Near Speech
House however an exciting art project adds to a forest walk and offers a
remarkable afternoon.

*Walk category* : Easy (2 hours).

*Length* : 8 km (5 miles).

*Ascent* :  60 m (200 ft).

*Maps* :  Landranger Sheet 162; Outdoor Leisure Sheet 14 (Wye Valley &
         Forest of Dean).

*Starting and finishing point* : There are car-parks at Speech House, at
622 122, and Beechenhurst, at 614 119, both on the B4226 Coleford to
Cinderford road. Use of the Beechenhurst site, which is not actually on
the route, adds around 500 m to the walk. Below, it is assumed that the
Speech House site will be used.

From the car-park take the marked route – the waymarking is by blue
ringed posts throughout – beyond the kissing gate, crossing the main
road to reach the forest. The route bends right to head north-east towards
Woorgreens Lake, once an open-cast mine, but now a nature reserve
renowned for its dragonflies and damselflies, and for the wildfowl that
use it for over-wintering or as a stop on the migration south. The site is
also home to both adders and grass snakes.
    The walk does not reach the lake, turning westward – at first north-
westward – after the first open-air sculpture is reached (see (1) Forest

# WALK 35   FOREST SCULPTURE

OLD RAILWAY TRACK (2)

N

WOORGREEN LAKE

(1)

(S)

P

KG

KG

P

SPEECH HOUSE (3)

½        1 k
     ½ m

sculpture). A stile is crossed before a long loop of pathway takes the
walker first southward then to the path's northern extremity. Here the
old forest railway is joined (see (2) Severn and Wye Railway), and
followed over three stiles until a cluster of sculptures is reached. At
these the old railway is left for another forest path, an out-and-back
diversion being necessary to reach sculpture 8A. When sculpture 10 is
reached the Walk is at its closest approach to the Beechenhurst car-park
and picnic site.

The B4226 is reached over a stile, and left by a path that circles the Speech House Hotel (see (3) Speech House) to rejoin the car-park starting point.

(1) *Forest sculpture*

The exhibition of permanently positioned sculptures in the forest was organised by the Arnolfini Gallery of Bristol in conjunction with the Forestry Commission. Additional funding has come from the Henry Moore Foundation, the Elephant Trust and the Carnegie United Kingdom Trust. The idea behind the exhibition was to commission artists to produce works that interpreted the forest. Each artist was given a site and produced a work that will remain *in situ* permanently. Indeed in the case of some of the works the use of natural materials means that they will eventually decay and are, therefore, a part of the 'living' fabric of the forest itself. In addition to the sculptures, some of which are startling, some amusing, but all thought-provoking, there are exhibitions of photography.

More sculptures are being commissioned, so it is not possible to give a complete list. A catalogue – in colour but with a subsidised and, as a result, an astonishingly low cover price – has been produced and is supplemented as more sculptures are added. The catalogue should be bought: not only will it enhance a walk around the exhibition, but will help finance future works. Some of the works have been vandalised, which is appalling. That is an easy comment to make, what is more difficult is to pick a favourite, indeed should a favourite be picked at all? Probably not, but I do like the stained glass of Keith Atherton – sculpture Number 1 – and the giant chair of Magdalene Jetelova, Number 9.

(2) *Severn and Wye Railway*

The Forest of Dean has long been a mining area. Coal is the most famous of the minerals mined, but iron ore was also worked extensively from the sixteenth to the nineteenth centuries. Building stone was quarried at several locations and limestone was crushed for agricultural lime. As elsewhere all early transportation was by pack-horse, but by the start of the 19th century tramways were being built. An early one was that linking the great waterways of the Severn and the Wye, opened in

1813 between Lydbrook and Lydney. This line had many side tracks to mines and quarries and was later taken over as a fully fledged railway carrying steam trains. A side line was also built to link it with Cinderford and on towards Gloucester. Our Walk along the old track is on the Cinderford link. Thanks to the great efforts of the Dean Forest Railway Preservation Society a section of the line, from Lydney to Parkend, is now open again with rides on old steam trains and a steam centre at Northend near Lydney. Parkend where the line stops, is about 6 km (4 miles) from Speech House.

### (3) *Speech House*

Prior to the Norman Conquest the Forest of Dean was, to all except those who lived in it, a curious, mysterious place, a wedge of densely afforested land between the Severn and the Wye in which lived solitary people making a living from charcoal burning or mining, their lives and interactions with each other and the outside world governed by a complex series of forest laws laid down, it would seem, in part to control exploitation of the forest itself, in part to prevent exploitation of themselves. The Norman kings changed all this by making the forest a Royal Forest, a hunting ground where the king alone had the right to kill. Penalties for poaching and for sheep grazing were high, but the charcoal burners and miners were not banished, just controlled. To exercise this control a system of officials was set up and these heard complaints and disputes at the Court of Verderers, a verderer being one who made a living from the *vert*, literally the green, the forest itself. The Court was held every forty days, and as it was also known as the Speech Court because of the rights to speech of the Verderers, it was held at the Speech House. The current house dates from the time of Charles II who used it as a hunting lodge. Speech House is now an hotel. The Court of Verderers is still held here, though no longer at forty day intervals, the courtroom, the timbered dining-room, being open to visitors.

   Beside the hotel, and also close to the starting car-park, is an arboretum with a good collection of both trees and shrubs.

Magdalene Jetelova's giant chair

## Walk 36 Lower Wye

In its lowest reaches the Wye Valley is well served with paths. The Offa's Dyke long-distance footpath joins it at Monmouth and travels down the left, the eastern, bank, while the (Lower) Wye Valley Walk links Hereford to Chepstow. From Ross to Redbrook the Valley Walk hops from bank to bank, but south of Redbrook it takes the right (western) bank. There is, therefore, the chance of a fine walk that is waymarked all along its length. If that walk joins Tintern to Chepstow it has the added advantage of visiting one of Britain's most beautifully set abbeys and one of its most commanding castles. Here, too, there is superb woodland and a collection of fine viewpoints.

*Walk category* : Difficult (5 hours).

*Length* : 20 km (12$^1/_2$ miles).

*Ascent* :  500 m (1650 ft).

*Maps* :  Landranger Sheet 162; Outdoor Leisure Sheet 14 (Wye Valley & Forest of Dean).

*Starting and finishing point* : Numerous, but the best ones are at the 'terminal' points, at Chepstow or, and better, at the car-park for Tintern Abbey on the A466 Chepstow to Monmouth road.

From the abbey car-park (see (1) Tintern Abbey) go right (north) along the main road for 250 m to a lane, left. Do not take this, but instead go hard left on a narrower lane – signed with the yellow arrow and yellow dot of the Wye Valley Walk – that runs back almost parallel to the main road. This lane rises steadily to reach woodland, continuing as a path through the woods to a stile and open countryside. Ahead is another piece of woodland through which a path threads its way to Wyndcliff (see (2) Wyndcliff). Here, having followed a road for a short section, the walk takes a track that reaches the car-park at the base of Wyndcliff, and continues out of the car-park on a track to the main A466. As an alternative to this route the 365 Steps can be used to descend to the base of Wyndcliff, an obvious path from the bottom of the steps being taken through some stunning woodland to the car-park. The Steps are not for the faint-hearted, one section climbing a near-vertical cliff by a staircase complete with wooden rungs. But there is a handrail. The Steps route is to be preferred, the cliffs of Wyndcliff offering fine views, while the boulders at their base offer good opportunities for the path to find an adventurous way.

Cross the A466 and continue on the waymarked path through Lower Martridge Wood and into what was once all Piercefield Park (see (3) Piercefield Park). When crossing the park the Wye Valley Walk stays among the trees bordering the race course. Pierce Wood is a delightful place, famous in a local story for having been dense enough to disorientate a Chepstow man, who, as dusk arrived, stood in the wood and shouted 'Man lost' with increasing despair. An owl in a nearby tree called 'whooo' and the man yelled 'The Clockmaker from Chepstow' in reply.

A wall in the wood is crossed by stile and soon after a short lane leads to a road. Go left and into Chepstow (see (4) Chepstow). Follow signs and the A48 to Chepstow Castle and cross the Wye beyond using the elegant but narrow bridge. At the end of the bridge the main road goes left, but we go ahead up a lane that cuts off the road's sweeping curve up Tutshill. Half-way up this lane the Offa's Dyke Path joins from the right and we follow its acorn signs to a point just above Tintern. Go over when the main road is regained, leaving the new road on a signed path that reaches the real dyke (see (5) Offa's Dyke) before going away from the river to traverse the backs of houses in Woodcroft village to reach Wintour's Leap (see (6) Wintour's Leap). Here the path rejoins the road, the B4228, and follows it around a sharp right-hand bend and on for 500 m around a left-hand bend. Just after Netherhope Lane has joined the road from the right, having come from Tidenham, a stone stile to the right gives access to a path. Follow it through Wallhope Grove and across open land to rejoin the B4228. Go right and follow the road for 800 m.

As Dennelhill Farm is approached the path goes left, leaving the road to enter the superb woodland of the Wye Valley's eastern bank. The path

TINTERN ⑦

TINTERN ABBEY ①

Ⓢ

500m

100m

150m

DEVIL'S PULPIT

200m

200m

OFFA'S DYKE

STEPS

WORGAN'S WOOD

DENNELHILL FARM

Ⓢ Ⓢ

50m

100m

Ⓢ

150m

200m

WYNDCLIFF ② 200m

WALK 36 LOWER WYE

uses steps to climb up into Boatwood Plantation but thereafter, in Worgan's Wood, the route follows the dyke itself as it contours around the valley side. At Plumweir Cliff the dyke turns sharp right, a turn made to maintain the contour, and continues to the rocky outcrop of the Devil's Pulpit. From here the Devil is said to have preached to the monks building Tintern Abbey, hoping to persuade them to stop their work. About 600 m after the Pulpit, at a sign for both the Pulpit and Brockweir, we leave the Offa's Dyke Path, going left on a path that drops down through the woods. Cross a forest track and continue down. Other paths join from the right, but the downhill route is obvious, leading to a cobbled track for a green lane. Go right, crossing the iron bridge over the Wye (see (7) Tintern) and going left beyond it to reach the abbey car-park.

## (1) *Tintern Abbey*

Tintern Abbey was one of the high spots of the Wye Tourer's journey, and this is no surprise, the abbey ruins being sufficiently complete to show how the building must have looked and to convey its beauty and yet being sufficiently ruinous and in such a delightful spot as to be truly romantic. The Revd William Gilpin, one of the most renowned Tourers, was a leading light of the movement that sought the Picturesque at places like Tintern Abbey. The seekers of the Picturesque roamed the country looking for views, which might even be looked at through a hand-held frame. Gilpin laid down the rules. 'Nature' he said, 'is always great in design ... but she is seldom so correct in composition, as to produce a harmonious whole.' A view, the good reverend gentleman explained, must have an 'area', two 'side-screens' and a 'front-screen'. Any view could, therefore, be marked out of ten for its composition. Low marks, presumably, made Nature blush with embarrassment. Gilpin found the abbey to be 'an elegant Gothick pile', but though he found parts beautiful, 'the whole is ill-shaped'. He decided that 'a mallet judiciously used (but who durst use it?) might be of service'.

The abbey was founded in 1131 for Cistercian monks, though what we see today derives almost entirely from a major rebuilding in the thirteenth century. The cloisters are later, probably from the fifteenth century. Little is known of the abbey's history as its records have not come down to us, but it can be assumed that the monks, certainly the early ones, were as industrious as all Cistercians were and had a major impact on the local economy. Henry VIII's Act of Dissolution was applied to Tintern in 1536 and the lead was stripped off the roof to expand the royal coffers. Devoid of their roofs all the dissolved abbeys decayed quickly. At Tintern the abbey fared better than elsewhere as there were fewer locals to plunder the ruins for building stone. What remains is a magnificent insight into early medieval architecture – the windows are the finest Gothic windows in Britain – and the monastic way of life. Please do take the time to visit.

(2) *Wyndcliff*

Wyndcliff is a fine outcrop of limestone set high above the Wye. At its top is a famous viewpoint known as the Eagle's Nest, from which the view is superb, one of the finest in the whole valley. From close to the Eagle's Nest the 365 Steps lead to the base of the cliff. They were constructed in 1828 by staff of the Duke of Beaufort after the area had become famous with lovers and other 'romantics' (poets and the like!). The steps were renovated in the early '70s by apprentices from the Beachley Army College. They did a fine job but reputedly reduced the number of steps to around 300. I have not counted to check, being confused, in truth, as to where step 1 is when approaching from the cliff base and usually being too engrossed in the view to be bothered.

(3) *Piercefield Park*

Piercefield Park was once the home of Valentine Morris who laid out a walk with ten viewpoints each supposed to embody the requirements of the Picturesque (see Note (1) above). Each viewpoint had a fanciful name - the Chinese Seat, the Grotto, the Druid's Temple – and they were constructed by a Chepstow-based landscape gardener. The layout cost Morris a fortune, the fortune his father had made from Antiguan sugar plantations. Morris's father also left him the plantations, the income from which Morris used to finance a lavish lifestyle. When, in 1770, giant ants ate the cane Morris was bankrupted and had to sell Piercefield to settle his debts. He left Chepstow for Antigua, and as he rode through the town the muffled church bell rang and crowds lined the streets. In the West Indies he revived his fortunes and was appointed Lieutenant General of St Vincent. He lost everything when the French invaded and despite the fact that he had financed a spirited defence from his own pocket, England's ungrateful government imprisoned him for bankruptcy. The injustice was never rectified and Morris died in poverty.

Later, before the race-course took over some of the parkland, the woods were famous for poachers. One was caught and taken to court in Chepstow. His defence was straightforward. 'Indeed your honour I never shot no pheasants at all. The only bird I shot was a rabbit, and I knocked that down with a stick.'

(4) *Chepstow*

The old Welsh name for the town was '*Ystraigyl* ', The Bend, from its position on the Wye. The Normans, when they came, used this name, calling their castle Striguil, but gradually the Saxon name – meaning market town, the prefix *cheap* for market also surviving in London's Cheapside and many villages with the word Chipping in their name – became the common form.

The castle dates from the eleventh century though most of what we now see is much later. It is a massive fortress, one of the most imposing in Britain, its huge walls sitting right on the Wye's sheer cliff. To add to the impressive nature of the castle the town walls, from the thriteenth century, are almost complete and have a fine gate, still used to take the traveller into the town. One member of the Norman de Clare family that held the castle for the king was Gilbert Strongbow, the surname deriving from his extraordinarily long and powerful arms. Gilbert also had five fingers (in addition to the thumb) on each hand, despite all of which he was 'a very perfect gentil knight'.

Gilbert was not at the castle when Edward II was held here before being taken to Berkeley Castle and his death, nor when Edward IV's father-in-law was held before being taken to Kenilworth Castle and execution. Later, during the second Civil War of 1648, there was death at the castle itself. It was held by Sir Nicholas Kemeys for the king. The Parliamentarians stormed the castle after an offer of terms had been refused. Many Royalists were killed, and a plaque marks the spot where Kemeys himself died. Later, with an irony lost on all at the time, the castle was the prison of Sir Henry Marten, one of those who had signed

Tintern Abbey

Charles I's death warrant. Marten, imprisoned after the Restoration, was unrepentant until his death. He is buried in the town church.

Visitors used to the Edwardian castles of North Wales will find Chepstow's long, narrow design strange, but there is no doubting the superb engineering of the site, and the views alone make a visit very worthwhile.

### (5) *Offa's Dyke*

The real reason for the construction of the dyke remains a mystery, the idea that it represents a defensive barrier against the marauding Celts occasionally losing ground to the idea that it was a negotiated political or trade boundary. Either way it was never completed, the final section to Prestatyn in North Wales being abandoned after Offa was killed in a battle with the Celts. Some say that the battle was over the line the final section should take which, if true, casts doubt on the negotiated boundary idea. Along its length the dyke is occasionally difficult to see, but in Worgan's Wood it is very obvious indeed, an eye-catching ridge from a distance, revealed as a huge rampart on closer inspection.

The Offa's Dyke long-distance footpath which our walk follows, if briefly, starts at Sedbury Cliffs on the Severn's banks near Chepstow and follows the line of the dyke, as far as is possible, all the way to Prestatyn.

### (6) *Wintour's Leap*

The huge, very steep and somewhat loose, limestone cliffs here are a favourite with rock climbers. They are named for Sir John Wintour, a Royalist who fortified his Lydney mansion and held it for the king during the Civil War. He was actually away from the house when a Parliamentarian army arrived, but his wife captained the guard on his behalf, and the Cromwellians withdrew, fed up with the struggle. Sir John was not at home because he was attempting to fortify the Severn banks at Beachley, aware that the river was easily crossed from here to Aust – a fact later used by a river ferry that was made redundant by the Severn Bridge. As Sir John and his men worked they were surprised by a Parliamentarian force and scrambled down the shallow cliffs to escape. Sir John's feat of scrambling down on horseback gave birth to a local

Winter sunset over the Wye from Wintour's Leap

legend that he had leapt these huge cliffs, and the cliffs were named in his honour. One look at the drop will dissuade the walker from the idea that Sir John leapt here.

## (7) *Tintern*

Tintern village grew up around the abbey, there being no authenticated history of occupation of the site before then, though the name derives from the Welsh Din Teyrn, from Dinas Teyrn, the fortress of Teyrn, king of Morgannwg – now Glamorgan. The legend has Teyrn being killed at a fortified site here, during a battle with Saxon invaders, at the end of the sixth century.

Following the dissolution of the abbey the village's fortunes declined, but there was a revival in the seventeenth century when the combination of local supplies of timber for charcoal, iron ore, and the river for transport, gave birth to an iron industry with furnaces beside the river. The local wire works was of great national importance and brass was made here for the first time in Britain. The iron bridge dates from this industrial era, the plate on it recalling that it once carried a tramway to the wire works.

# Appendices

*Offa's Dyke Path*
The Offa's Dyke Path is one of the two official long-distance footpaths
to cross southern Wales. It starts (or ends) at Sedbury Cliffs on the
eastern bank of the River Severn a little way from Chepstow. From there
it follows the eastern bank of the River Wye – Walk 36 follows part of
the Path here – to Monmouth from where it heads westward to the
Brecon Beacons National Park. It follows the extreme western ridge of
the Black Mountains, passing above Llanthony Priory to reach Hay
Bluff. From there it descends to Hay-on-Wye. It goes north to Kington,
taking the eastern edge of the Radnor Forest to Knighton and going
across the Clun Forest to Montgomery, and on to Welshpool. Northward
it leaves the area covered by this book as it heads for its terminal town of
Prestatyn.

   See *Offa's Dyke Path* , Christopher John Wright, a Constable Guide.

*The Pembrokeshire Coastal Path*
The Pembrokeshire Coastal Path traverses the  Coast National Park from
St. Dogmael's in the north – on the old county boundary between
Pembrokeshire and Cardiganshire – to Amroth in the south – on the old
county boundary between Pembrokeshire and Carmarthenshire.
Throughout its 295 km (184 miles) length it hugs the coast except where
danger areas or industrial sites force it inland. Walks 10, 12(a) and 12(b)
follow sections of the path.

   See *Pembrokeshire Coast Path*, Christopher John Wright, a Constable
Guide.

*The Cambrian Way*
Despite strenuous efforts by the Countryside Commission to find a
pathway through the conflicting desires of walkers' interest groups,
countryside interest groups and farmers, the attempt to produce a
Cambrian Way was finally abandoned in 1982. The route was to have
started in Cardiff, moving north through Risca and Pontypool to

Blaenafon. From Blorenge Mountain it was to have descended to the Monmouthshire and Brecon Canal, going westward along it to reach Llangattock and the escarpment above it, or, as an option, going north to Abergavenny and taking a horseshoe across the Black Mountains. From the Llangattock Escarpment the route was to have gone west, crossing the Brecon Beacons and Forest Fawr to Mynydd Ddu. Beyond Llyn y Fan Fach it would have gone north to Llandovery and Rhandirmwyn, then north again across Elenydd and Plynlimon to Machynlleth and the Snowdonia National Park. After traversing all the main ranges of the Park the Way would have finished in Conway.

A guide to a personal interpretation of this route has been published by the author of this guide – see *A Cambrian Way*, Richard Sale, a Constable Guide.

*Owain Glyndwr's Way*
This 200 km (125 mile) path was established by Powys County Council and is maintained and waymarked by them. It starts at Knighton and moves west across fields and moorland to Abbey Cwmhir, then goes northward to Llanidloes. From the town it crosses the Severn and heads north-west to Dylife from where Walk 3 follows the Way to the flank of Foel Fadian. The Way itself descends to Machynlleth – scene of a Glyndwr Parliament – and then turns east, following the Dyfi valley, then going east again to Llanbrynmair. Northward it reaches Lake Vyrnwy before it turns east to go across beautiful country to reach Welshpool. Since Knighton and Welshpool are both on the Offa's Dyke Path a circular route is possible.

A guide book to the route by the author of this guide is to be published shortly as a Constable Guide.

*Wye Valley Walks*
In its upper section the Wye Valley is followed by a route from Rhayader to Hay-on-Wye, a 55 km (35 mile) waymarked path. Walk 33 follows a section of this path. In its lower section the (Lower) Wye Valley Walk follows the river from Hereford to Chepstow offering, in its final stretch, an alternative to the Offa's Dyke Path that follows the opposite bank. Walks 34 and 36 follow sections of this lower path.

A guide book to these routes, indeed to the whole valley, has been published by the author of this guide – see *The Wye Valley*, Richard Sale, Wildwood House (soon to be re-published).

*Usk Valley Walk*
Gwent County Council have waymarked and maintain a path that follows the River Usk from Caerleon to Abergavenny. A series of route cards for this fine route is available.

*Other short walks*
There are numerous Forestry Commission forests in the area covered by this book, and many of these have short forest or nature trails set out through them. Leaflets on these are available from the Forest Centres set up in several of the larger forests.

In addition the Brecon Beacons National Park Committee offer a superb series of guided walks in the summer months, explaining all aspects of the Park. Information on these can be obtained from the Park Office, see '*Useful Addresses*' below. Facilities for disabled visitors and walkers are available. Please contact the Park Information Offices.


APPENDIX 2 TRANSPORT AND WEATHER

Over such a wide area it is not possible to be definitive about the transport that is, or will be, available. The local information centres will have such information.

*Weather Reports*
A weather report for the Brecon Beacons National Park is available by dialling 0898 500414.

One for the Pembrokeshire Coast National Park is available by dialling Saundersfoot 0834 812516.

APPENDIX 3 USEFUL ADDRESSES

*Brecon Beacons National Park*

National Park Office
7 Glamorgan Street
Brecon
Powys LD3 7DP
Tel: Brecon (0874) 4437

Mountain Centre
Nr. Libanus
Brecon
Powys LD3 8ER
Tel: Brecon (0874) 3366

*Information Centres*

| | |
|---|---|
| Abergavenny | Tel: (0873) 3254 |
| Craig-y-Nos Country Park | Tel: (0639) 730395 |
| Brecon | Tel: (0874) 611316 |
| Llandovery | Tel: (0550) 20693 |

*Pembrokeshire Coast National Park*

National Park Information Officer
County Offices
Haverfordwest
Dyfed SA61 1QZ
Tel: Haverfordwest (0437) 764591

*Information Centres*

| | |
|---|---|
| Broad Haven | Tel: (0437) 781412 |
| Haverfordwest | Tel: (0437) 66141 |
| Kilgetty | Tel: (0834) 812175 |
| Newport, Dyfed | Tel: (0239) 820912 |

| | |
|---|---|
| Pembroke | Tel: (0646) 682148 |
| St David's | Tel: (0437) 720392 |
| Tenby | Tel: (0834) 2402 |

*Other Organisations*

Cadw (Welsh Historical Monuments)
Brunel House
2 Fitzalan Road
Cardiff
South Glamorgan CF2 1UY
Tel: (0222) 465511

Countryside Commission
John Dower House
Crescent Place
Cheltenham
Glos GL50 3RA
Tel: (0242) 21381

Countryside Commission
Welsh Office
Ladywell House
Newtown
Powys SV16 1JB
Tel: (0686) 26799

Forestry Commission
Victoria Terrace
Aberystwyth
Dyfed SY23 2DQ
Tel: (0970) 612367

National Trust
36 Queen Anne's Gate
London SW1H 9AS
Tel: (01) 222 9251

National Trust
South Wales Office
King's Head
Bridge Street
Llandeilo
Dyfed SA19 6BN
Tel: (0558) 822000

Nature Conservancy Council
Plas Gogerddan
Aberystwyth
Dyfed SY23 3EB
Tel: (0970) 820295

Offa's Dyke Association
Old Primary School
West Street
Knighton
Powys LD7 1EW
Tel: (0547) 528753

Royal Society for the Protection of Birds
Bryn Aderyn
The Bank
Newtown
Powys SV16 2AB
Tel: (0686) 626678

Wales Tourist Board
South Wales Regional Office
Ty Croeso
Gloucester Place
Swansea
West Glamorgan SA1 1TY
Tel: (0792) 465204

# Index